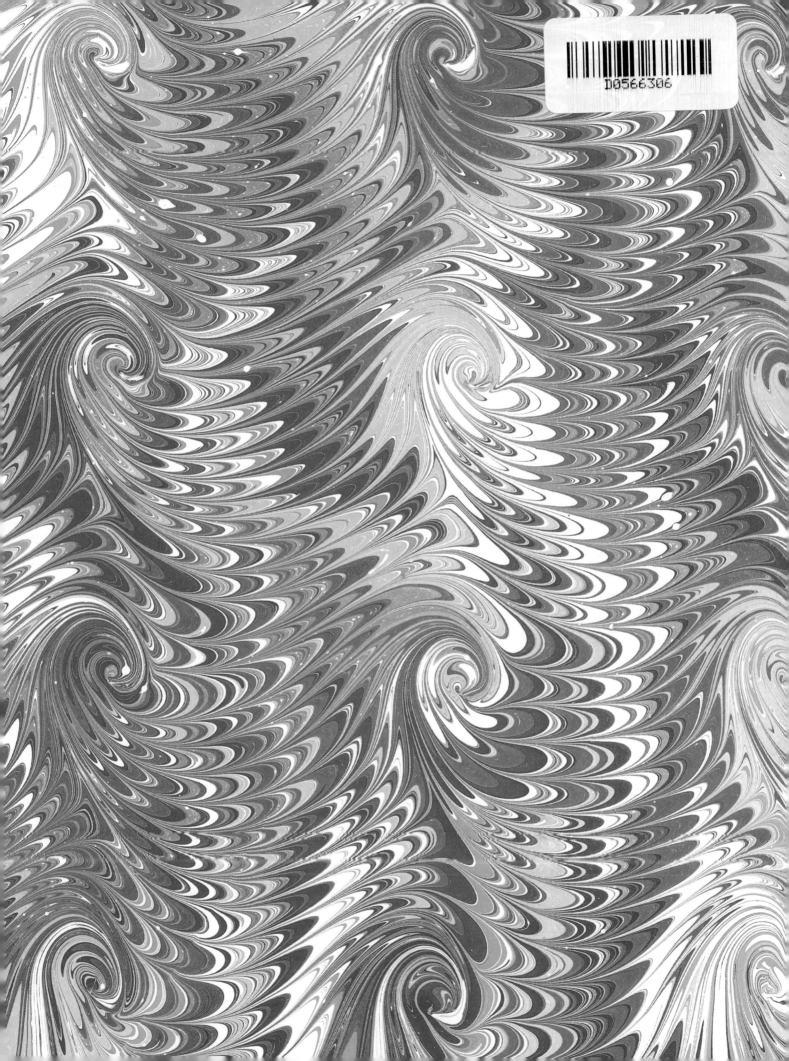

Collecting Noritake, A to Z

Art Deco & More

A Pictorial Record and
Guide to Values

David Spain

Schiffer
Publishing Ltd

4880 Lower Valley Road, Atglen, PA 19310 USA

I dedicate this book to my good friends Sheldon and
Sayo Harmeling, Noritake collectors extraordinary.
Two finer people you will not meet.

Copyright © 1999 by David Spain
Library of Congress Catalog Card Number: 98-87929

Designed by Bonnie M. Hensley
Type set in Garamond Bk BT/Times New Roman

ISBN: 0-7643-0740-1
Printed in China
1 2 3 4

Published by Schiffer Publishing Ltd.
4880 Lower Valley Road
Atglen, PA 19310
Phone: (610) 593-1777; Fax: (610) 593-2002
E-mail: Schifferbk@aol.com

In Europe, Schiffer books are distributed by Bushwood Books
6 Marksbury Rd. Kew Gardens
Surrey TW9 4JF England
Phone: 44 (0)181 392-8585; Fax: 44 (0)181 392-9876
E-mail: Bushwd@aol.com

Please visit our web site catalog at www.schifferbooks.com or write for a free catalog. This book may be
purchased from the publisher. Please include $3.95 for shipping. Please try your bookstore first. We are
interested in hearing from authors with book ideas on related subjects.

Contents

Acknowledgments

This book is the product of the hard work and high interest of many Noritake collectors and dealers from all parts of the United States as well as Canada, England and Japan. Without their help, I could not have completed this book. Of the many who have helped in one way or another, I begin with a note of special gratitude directed to those whose *exceptional* photographic efforts have contributed so much to making this book a reality: Melissa Arenson, Judi Camero, Sheldon Harmeling, Margaret Anderson Hetzler, Gary Kaufman, Bob Suslowicz and Bob Trennert. Each went the proverbial "extra mile" in order to let us see how beautiful Noritake collectibles really are. For fine photographs provided by others, I also wish to thank Cindy Babcock, Doug and Donna Bingaman, Michael Conrad, Alec Cooper, Jean Dillard, Dana Dwaileebe, Joane McCaslin Ferguson, Greg Heiden, Brian Hurst, Dale and Lou Knight, Mike Kocor, Diane Kovarik, Dick Nelson, Bill and Christopher Phillipson, Hank Sasaki, and Tim Trapani.

In my travels seeking Noritake to photograph, I was shown wonderful, almost boundless hospitality by various fellow collectors, most of whom I had known, until then, primarily through phone conversations, correspondence and collector conventions. In this regard, I am particularly grateful to Tom and Gerri Seitz and to Norm and Lida Derrin for letting me stay with them for extended periods on a recent photo safari "back East." "Above and beyond the call of duty" does not begin to suggest the extent of their efforts. My memories of my stay with them are fond indeed. For truly gracious and much appreciated hospitality of other kinds on that and other recent trips, I want to thank the following collectors: Christel A. Bachert, Susan Buonafede, Deirdre Cimianio, Lisa and Gary Gibson, Bonnie and Dewaine Glyda, Leslie and Mike Iarusso, Gary Kaufman, Rhonda and John Perroncino, Marlene and Michael Rosen, Rita Rosso, Earl and Roberta Sloboda, Janet and Tim Trapani, and Joe and Rhoda Westler. For similar hospitality, I also am indebted to my good friends Tony Chu and Amy Lee, Dorothy Rose Hauk, Jan and Ed MacEwen, Deborah Pellow and Cathy Tiao and Jimmy Fu as well as my cousin Alice Polley and my parents, Norman and Ruth Spain.

Collectors tend to be very protective of their collections, especially when they are fragile and valuable. Yet, many Noritake collectors permitted me to come into their homes to handle and photograph their precious pieces. That they have been so willing to allow this says a great deal about their enthusiasm for their hobby. I will always be so very grateful to all who have let me disrupt their lives in this way—specifically, David Abramson, Christel A. Bachert, Donna and Doug Bingaman, Dr. Dennis and Susan Buonafede, Gary and Joanna Goodman, Kimberly Carman, Deirdre Cimiano, Claire and Michael Conrad, Marilyn Derrin, Norm and Lida Derrin, Jean and Joe Dillard, Patricia Engel, Rosemary Farrell, Joane and Bruce Ferguson, Lisa and Gary Gibson, Dewaine and Bonnie Glyda, Leslie Iarusso, Sheldon and Sayo Harmeling, Bob and Bernadette Jackson, Gary Kaufman, Laurie Larson, Joe and Deanna Liotta, Jim Martin, Dick and Sally Nelson, Mike and Connie Owen, Rhonda and John Perroncino, Mike and Marlene Rosen, Robert and Rita Rosso, Earl and Roberta Sloboda, Earl Smith and Mark Griffin, Bob Suslowicz, Fred Tenney, Tim and Janet Trapani, Bob and Linda Trennert, Dennis and Lori Trishman, Rhoda and Joe Westler, and Nancy and Charlie Wilson. In what can only be described as acts of trust and daring, which I have always found touching, some collectors and dealers have actually brought or sent pieces to me to photograph. For such efforts, I am deeply grateful to Donna and George Avezzano, Carrie and Gerry Domitz, Mary Lou Gross, Diane Kovarik, Janet and Ken Lodge, Pat Leon, Jim Martin, Chloe McKinney and Dick Nelson.

I have received moral and other comparable forms of support and encouragement from many friends, of whom I name here only a few that inadvertently were not mentioned at the outset of my first book on Noritake collectibles: Sharon Burgett, Jim and Jaw-Ing Chow, John Narver and Steve, Gunnel, Elise and Anna Tanimoto. For their able assistance in helping me record vital information about the pieces as I was photographing them, I want to thank, in addition to virtually everyone named above, Miss Carly Derrin (V.280 is especially for you, Carly), Master Grant Gibson and Miss Rachel Spain. My then-thirteen year-old daughter also deserves credit for taking the photo of me that was on the dust jacket of my first book on Noritake collectibles. Another one was used in this book, as well. For able assistance of other kinds, I heartily thank Bill Strohl of Exit 21 Antiques in Pennsylvania. For expert and, most of all, patient and understanding efforts in processing, printing, reprinting and re-re-printing literally thousands of photos for me, I thank Roseann Kautz and Chris Sturgul of the Broadway Film Stop, and Maggie McKnight of Costco Store No. 1—all in Seattle.

I also want to thank, for their continuing support, in various ways, my author friends Lou Ann Donahue, Joan Van Patten and Carole Bess White, my Noritake Company friends Mr. Keishi Suzuki and Bill Donahue, and my dealer friends Dennis and Diane Burnickas, Norm Derrin, Carrie and Gerry Domitz, Brian and Yvonne Hurst, Pat and Dave Leon, Doris and George Myers and Chloe McKinney (among others).

As for my wife Jannie and daughter Rachel (as well as the rest of my family), no attempt to put into words my feelings of high regard and deep love could ever be adequate or sufficient. Even so, I must say here as I did in my first Noritake book: but for their love, support and patience, this book would not exist.

Part One

Chapter 1
Aims and Scope of This Book

This book follows up on themes and materials introduced in my first book on Noritake collectibles (*Noritake Collectibles A to Z*), published in 1997. It was then and still is the largest and most comprehensive book in the field, with over 1200 color photos, but it only scratched the surface of what is "out there." This second book adds over 550 photographs to that record, but the surface still has only a slightly deeper scratch (an awful metaphor for a collector of porcelain to use, come to think of it). I have well over a thousand photos in hand that I have not yet documented in a book such as this one and there are more on the way.

This corpus is huge, even though this book is not about *all* the many varieties of decorative porcelains ever made by the Noritake Company. To record that output would require *many* volumes indeed. Instead, this book, like my previous one on the subject, focuses on non-dinnerware porcelains (except for the Azalea, Roseara, Tree-in-the-Meadow and "Howo" patterns) made and decorated by the Noritake Company, as evidenced by backstamps containing the words "Noritake" and "Japan" or "Made in Japan" (with a few exceptions discussed below in the section of this chapter dealing with backstamps). Excluded are Noritake Company porcelains with backstamps containing the word "Nippon," except when it occurs in the phrase "Nippon Toki Kaisha," which means, in essence, Japanese Ceramics Company.

Most of the items shown in this book were made prior to 1940; indeed, most were made in the 1920s. A few of the items in this book (there were more in the previous one) may have been made as long ago as 1908; others are more recent (in this book, up to the late 1970s). Also, most were made for export, by-and-large to the United States, but also to Great Britain and other countries of the Commonwealth. In addition, there are items with backstamps indicating they were intended for the domestic (i.e., Japanese) market. For more on this, see Chapter 3.

This book has two parts. If you are typical, you have already looked at Part Two. That is where nearly all of the color photos are found. Photos are grouped into 12 chapters with names and alphabetic designations designed to facilitate the location of particular items. How this works is discussed a bit more in the Introduction to Part Two. Part One has three chapters. In the first one, I do two things. First, I indicate how the book is organized. Second, I note what its scope is. In Chapter 2, I discuss Art Deco styles, in general and as they may be found on Noritake porcelains. In Chapter 3, I briefly review, in a non-technical manner, a little of the available information about backstamps and other "marks" that are usually but not always on the bottom of Noritake porcelains. Table 3.1 summarizes this material, including important updated information from the Noritake Company regarding backstamp registration dates.

The scope of this book is the same as my previous book on Noritake collectibles. This scope, I feel it is important to emphasize, was set largely *for*, rather than *by*, me. It mostly reflects matters over which I had little or no control. One such factor, and in many ways the most important one, has to do with the interests of people who call themselves "Noritake collectors." The other two factors are what are sometimes referred to as "accidents" of history—i.e., events (whether planned or not) that shape the future or the course of history, even if there is no particular rational reason that this should have been the case.

The first "accident of history" grew out of American and British laws regulating the importing of goods from foreign countries. These laws established how the country of origin was to be indicated on imported items. Prior to 1921, the word "Nippon" had been used by virtually all Japanese companies to label their exports to the United States. "Nippon" is the English rendering of the *Japanese* name for the country we know as "Japan." In the United States, after 1921, the country of origin had to be the *English* version of the country's name. This meant that, after 1921, imported goods could no longer bear the word "Nippon." Instead, the word "Japan" or the words "Made in Japan" had to be used. At about the same time, the word "Noritake" also began to be incorporated into the identifying backstamps for Noritake Company goods exported to the United States.

As it happens, however, the Noritake Company treated differently the porcelains destined for Great Britain, even though its laws regarding the name of the country of origin were similar to those in the United States. Specifically, backstamps with the words "Noritake" (rather than no explicit company name) and "Japan" or "Made in Japan" (rather than "Nippon") appeared as early as 1908 on products exported to Great Britain. This was more than ten years earlier than was the case for similar goods destined for the United States. We will return to this point shortly. First, however, we need to consider the second historical accident.

This "accident" has to do with largely unplanned differences in the history of "Nippon" and "Noritake" collecting in the United States. By the early 1970s, in the United

States, porcelains marked with the word "Nippon" (meaning, in effect, "Made in Japan") were being collected seriously by a fairly sizable number of people. Newsletters for Nippon collectors were published and, by the last years of that decade, interest was sufficient to warrant the publishing of the first high quality book on the subject: Joan Van Patten's *Collector's Encyclopedia of Nippon* (1979). Two years later, Nippon collectors, by this time organized as the International Nippon Collectors Club (INCC), began to hold an annual convention. INCC members were and still are united by several things. One of the most important is their interest in porcelains with the word "Nippon" in the backstamp—so long as it appeals to their tastes and budgets, of course. The collecting interests of individual INCC members do vary, of course—sometimes greatly. Some have very wide interests; others have interests that are much more precisely defined. Many are oriented to one or two decorative styles (e.g., Art Nouveau) or, even, to particular motifs (e.g., airplanes or geese), colors (e.g., cobalt) or surface treatments (tapestry or coralene). This is still true to this day. It should be emphasized, however, that many of these collectors did and still do strongly favor items made by the Noritake Company, both because such items are apparently more plentiful and because the porcelains they made (then as now) were so often of much higher quality.

For various reasons, relatively few INCC members were interested in Japanese porcelains marked "Noritake." Most assuredly, however, this is not to say that "Noritake" collectibles were unknown to Nippon collectors. Indeed, several pioneer Noritake collectors (e.g., the late Viola Breves and Rita Gillis, as well as Norm Derrin, Fred Tenney and Marilyn Derrin, among others) were *centrally* involved with the activities of the INCC. Indeed, in 1984, Joan Van Patten, herself one of the founders of the INCC, published her first book on Noritake collectibles, *The Collectors Encyclopedia of Noritake*. Nippon Club members provided many of the photographs in it. Prior to this, however, two other individuals had published books on "Noritake Made in Japan" porcelains. The first to do so was Lou Ann Donahue who, in 1979, published a small but important book on her interests, *Noritake Collectibles*. Although the title refers only to Noritake, it is significant that she included *both* "Nippon" and "Noritake" collectibles in it. It is, so far, the only American book covering both of these collecting areas equally, although two such books have been published in Japan.

The second Noritake-collecting pioneer to bring widespread public attention to this collecting interest was the late Howard Kottler. In a booklet published in 1982, in connection with a traveling exhibit of a fragment of his by then huge collection of Art Deco Noritake, *Noritake Art Deco Porcelains,* Kottler notes that he began to collect Noritake seriously in 1970 (see Kottler, 1982, p.31). In contrast to Donahue, Kottler's booklet focused exclusively on Art Deco Noritake. Neither Donahue nor Kottler, it is important to note, was involved in any significant way with a Noritake

or Nippon collector group when they published their books. Not until the very late 1980s, in fact, were there more than subtle hints that the collecting of porcelains marked with the words "Japan" and "Noritake" might see growth that was anything like what had happened in the "Nippon" field 15 years before.

One of these developments was the launching, in 1989, of *Noritake News*, a quarterly newsletter for collectors of and dealers in Noritake as well as other Japanese porcelain collectibles. This was followed, in 1994, by the formation of the Noritake Collectors' Society (for information about *Noritake News* or the Society, write to the author c/o Schiffer Publishing). As with the INCC, the members of the Noritake Collectors' Society (NCS) have varied collecting interests. There are some, for example, who define their interests in terms of one or another decorative style. Some might emphasize items with Art Deco characteristics, while others might prefer, say, pieces in a Tree-in-the-Meadow style. Some prefer certain kinds of items (e.g., bowls or vases), while others might prefer certain motifs (e.g., birds, cottages or florals). In this, NCS members are very much like the members of the INCC.

In addition to preferring porcelains of different styles, there is one other way the two groups do differ, and this bears directly on how the scope of this book was established. The NCS is oriented to the products of a particular *company* whereas the INCC is oriented to the products of a particular *country*. Thus, any member of the INCC is likely to be at least somewhat fascinated by any porcelain with the word "Nippon" in the backstamp. Similarly, any member of the NCS is likely to be at least somewhat fascinated by any porcelain with the word "Noritake" in the backstamp. The membership of the sets of people who collect these two kinds of porcelains overlaps, but only slightly. In the course of events, each set has formed its own organization, established its own newsletter and organized its own annual convention. The scope of this book reflects these facts of collector preferences and organizational distinctions.

This viewpoint, which I have characterized as an "accident of history," is, however, more-or-less distinctly North American. This is because, as previously noted, the backstamps on Noritake Company porcelains exported to England early in this century used the word "Noritake" and did not use the word "Nippon." That is why, when I began to plan my first Noritake book, the scope was expanded beyond the traditional (in North America) 1921–1941 definition of the Noritake range. In doing this, I also and at once achieved another of my goals: to include materials pertaining to the full range of Noritake collecting interests to which those in all parts of the world who called themselves "Noritake collectors" were committed. All of this also explains, at least partly, why I went into so much detail in that first book about who Noritake collectors were, what they collected and how these facts were linked to the scope of that book. All of that applies to this book as well.

Chapter 2

Absorbing Styles:
Searching for Art Deco in Noritake Fancy Line Porcelains

It is not entirely unintentional that the first two words of this chapter title are a bit enigmatic. My aim in using them, however, is to do more than puzzle readers. Rather, they point to two of the more basic points that I wish to make here. Because of this, I begin this essay with a few comments about them, starting with the word "styles." Its plural form looks innocent enough, but its use here is a statement of some importance to me. With it, I call attention to a perhaps necessary but still potentially misleading convention in the way people write about Art Deco.

Generally, in the literature on Art Deco, one sees the word "style" used in its singular form. Indeed, I myself am guilty of this "sin." In a previous essay on this subject, I used the singular "style," not only throughout the essay but also in the title itself ("Searching for Art Deco Noritake and the Elements of a Style," see *bibliography* for details). I did this, I like to think, not out of ignorance but, rather, because it is difficult (at least in English) to use the plural when writing about those diverse strands of artistic thought and action, which, together, constitutes Art Deco. So, let me be clear about one thing right away: no matter how often one sees the word "style" used in the singular in this book, and especially in this essay, Art Deco is *not* a single homogeneous thing. It is, rather, a many-splendored thing.

When I (and others) refer to Art Deco as "a" style, this is not unlike saying that Art Deco is like "a" language. And, insofar as this is true, then it also is being said, although tacitly for the most part, that a complete analysis ought to give as much attention to what are thought of as its dialects as to whatever one takes to be its classic, mainstream form. (I am, by the way, both well aware of *and sympathetic to* the arguments of those who see many deep problems in saying that there is a classical or mainstream form of something like a language. Given the more limited purposes of this essay, I believe it is preferable to leave those issues for another day.) Thus, although some comments will be made about the general character of Art Deco as a style, I by no means intend a "complete analysis." Instead, my goal, here and in the introductions to several of the chapters of Part Two of this book, is to provide a basis for appreciating one of Art Deco's very interesting "dialects"—namely, Art Deco as manifested in Noritake fancy line porcelains of the 1920s.

The subject of language as analogous to Art Deco as a style is relevant also to the first word of the title ("Absorbing"), which is meant to be read in two ways. First, I use this word to acknowledge that Art Deco is an "absorbing"— i.e., an interesting—subject, a claim that Art Deco fans would accept readily, of course. Second, but far more substantially, I use it to point to another key theme of this es-

say—namely, that we learn about an art style much as we learn a (first or subsequent) language: we "absorb" it by immersing ourselves in it. This is *not* to say that we can't be aided in this effort by formal instruction. Such efforts can be and usually are vital. Even so, there is no substitute for being exposed to *many* examples of what one is trying to understand. This book provides the opportunity for such exposure because *many* examples of Art Deco Noritake are shown in it. Since, however, there also are many non-Art Deco items in this book, it cannot be assumed that one unfamiliar with the style can absorb it simply by gazing long and hard at all the works shown in Part Two. Indeed, this would be true even if Part Two contained nothing but Art Deco works, since one still would need at least some guidance regarding what particular things one ought to look for out of the myriad possible things one could note.

This is what prompts every art historian I have ever known to want to teach those interested in a given style by showing and discussing example after example after example and, on occasion, "non-examples," which instruct, as it were, by contrast. The temptation is great, but I cannot provide this sort of exposure in a brief essay such as this one. In other words, I cannot write about every item in this book that might usefully tell the interested reader what Art Deco is or is not, as a style.

There is more to this decision than the matter of the essay's length, however. This takes us again to the way Art Deco as a style can be compared to a language. There is more to learning a language than memorizing lists of words and grammatical rules. The real aim is to be able to *use* the words and rules to create and understand *new* sentences— even sentences that have never been uttered before. This sort of knowing is not a simple process. It involves repeated excursions from the classroom, where the vocabulary and grammar of useful examples are discussed, into the wider world where one will be exposed, it is hoped, to things that may or may not be examples of what one is trying to understand. By the same token, the undiscussed examples in this book represent an essential opportunity for the reader to evaluate the "Deco-ness" of items independently.

If you have ever learned a second language after about the age of 15, you will know that this process can be difficult and filled with sometimes embarrassing and usually funny failures. But, as any experienced teacher can attest, one of the best ways for us to learn is to pay attention to our failures. Pre-toddlers who want to walk will fall many times. To master the art of walking, they have to get up and try again and again and again. They cannot simply sit and think about what went wrong; they must, at some point, engage in real-world efforts to walk. It is the same with language learning. Learning ever longer vocabulary lists and increasingly arcane grammatical rules will not, by itself, do the trick. There is no getting around it: you have to get out there and try talking and listening, again and again.

Even though it is difficult and, at times, frustrating (as well as embarrassing), this sort of learning (whether of a language or an art style) can be exciting. Indeed, it is more than this; it is liberating. It permits one to be creative and to understand novelty that occurs within the rules that define and delimit a style or language. Thus, my hope is that the few comments presented here and in the chapter introductions about a small sampling of the Art Deco items shown in this book will enable you to look at and appreciate all Art Deco Noritake, whether in your own collection or the collections of others, or in books like this one.

This having been said, it may now more meaningfully, I hope, be noted that the first two words of the title signal that this essay (and its extensions in the chapter introductions of Part Two) is about four things: (1) Art Deco as an absorbing subject, which (2) one must learn about, much as one learns (or absorbs) a language and (3) Art Deco generally as a multi-stranded bundle of styles along with (4) Art Deco as manifested in Noritake fancy line porcelains of the 1920s.

I Know What I Like

"I may not know much about art, but I do know what I like." This overused sentiment, I freely admit, applied to me when I first began collecting Noritake. I knew I liked Art Deco Noritake. I also knew I was having reasonable success picking out Art Deco pieces from the mixed array I saw at shows and in shops. At the same time, however, I knew I could say very little about what the grounds were for granting a piece of Noritake the revered title "Deco." Like swimming or riding a bicycle, collecting Art Deco Noritake was, for me, a lot easier to do than to talk about. This, I like to think, points to the more benign meaning of the phrase at the start of this paragraph. It serves to remind us of the difference between "knowing" and "knowing about" something. You *know* computer problems when your PC will not boot up (as mine would not when I first sat down to write this chapter—really!); it takes a computer technician (or a teenager) to know *about* computer problems. Similarly, many collectors and dealers definitely *know* Art Deco wares when they see them. Indeed, they will knock down good friends in their efforts to get to them first. Apparently, though, it takes a specialist to know *about* Art Deco.

If it is presumed that one must be an art historian to qualify as the needed specialist, then I most certainly do not fit the bill for I am merely a collector. As such, my goal has always been simple: to find and, if I could afford it, buy Art Deco porcelains made by the Noritake Company. Intuition was the foundation of my early efforts to achieve this goal. I did reasonably well, at first. Eventually, however, I began to realize I was making more than a few of the only

two mistakes one *can* make. I either did not buy things I later knew I should have or I bought things I later realized I should not have. That's when I decided it was time to do a little homework. I offer some of the results of that effort here. The outcome, as I see it, is anything but "the" definitive treatise on "Deco" as an artistic tradition. Neither is it an attempt to convince collectors that they should not go out on "the hunt" until they have memorized and can flawlessly recite, chapter and verse, "Spain's Eight Rules" (or whatever the number might be) for identifying "genuine" Art Deco Noritake. Rather, I hope my observations about Art Deco as a style will seem reasonable enough to justify incorporating them into your outlook as a collector or dealer. As such, these views should become no more than a *part* of the assessment process that any collector uses when faced with the opportunity to buy, sell or, simply, enjoy looking at Noritake porcelain.

The Historical Roots of Art Deco

At the outset of this essay, I stated that Art Deco was not a single thing but, rather, a *set* of distinguishable, if not always completely distinctive, art styles. This is demonstrated in many ways, not least being what is generally accepted regarding the origins of this style. Thus, art historians and other experts have shown that the roots of Art Deco extend to the turn of the twentieth century and the efforts of creative individuals in many nations. A typical list of the leading countries in this regard, *not* in order of importance and not definitively, would include Austria, France, Germany, Great Britain, Holland, Italy, Russia and the United States. Now think about it: on how much did individuals in those countries, whether artists or not, agree at the turn of the century or, more specifically, by 1914? Is it any wonder, then, that leading-edge artistic endeavors within those nations should seem distinctive when considered comparatively?

At the same time, however, this does not mean there are no common elements or themes within this diversity, especially when viewed retrospectively. Although stylistic coherence may well be something the present too often imposes on the past, this does not mean there never has been coherence. Whether there was or not is really more of an empirical matter than a philosophical one. There are, of course, several logical possibilities. Past coherence may have gone unrecognized, it may have been denied (and often for nationalistic reasons) or it may have been claimed even when, from our vantage point, we can find none. One must remain open about this until one has looked into it.

When I look into it, I see coherence, which is by no means equivalent to saying that I see uniformity. This coherence exists, I believe, because that collection of distinct yet related artistic styles known collectively today as "Art Deco" originated in the midst of an array of *formative* technological and social developments. These first occurred, primarily in Europe and America, a century ago. One may gain at least a sense of the character of these developments by recalling the monumental and, often, profoundly disturbing ideas contained in the work of individuals as diverse as Einstein, Freud, Marx (via Lenin), Picasso, Shaw, Edison and Ford, among others. They all, it seems to me, questioned the unquestionable; indeed, they did more than this: they *effectively* questioned it (for many do this ineffectively all the time). Their work undermined, profoundly, what the vast majority in their day believed were timeless verities. Because of their revolutionary ideas, we literally see the world differently than did those who came before these intellectual giants were on the scene. Relativity, sex and the unconscious, political revolution, Cubism and "the primitive," cynicism (especially about what the majority continued to see as "proper"), days extended into incandescent nights (i.e., nights shortened by incandescent lights) and mass-production assembly lines are but a few of the thought-transforming developments introduced during the last decade of the nineteenth century and the first of the twentieth. It was a time when the mighty but ponderous engines of the early days of the industrial revolution of a century before began to reach previously unimagined speeds and to harness astoundingly large amounts of energy. On the domestic front, seemingly timeless axioms about homes and families, gender and role, dress and etiquette, social and political life—all were in flux.

Artists were hardly immune to such developments; indeed, the traditional view is that they contributed directly to the fostering of them (and, obviously, two of the great revolutionaries in the list above *were* artists). Many were quite consciously attempting to shed what they saw as the threadbare assumptions of their predecessors. Italian "Futurists" were, collectively, one of the more dramatic examples. Founded in 1909 by artists from in and around Milan, they wrote "manifestos" in which, among other things, they compared the great art museums of Italy to mausoleums and called for their destruction. They embraced new technologies with great passion. They lionized speed, efficiency and power particularly. Ironically, and to the consternation and embarrassment of many later on, such themes and, hence, this artistic movement, appealed to Mussolini and many other Italian Fascists.

In Russia, at about the same time, a movement with kindred energies and outlook emerged in the context of the Bolshevik Revolution. Known as Constructivism, the artists and architects in this movement produced works that were intended not only to agitate but also to propagandize. A leading center of this effort was what had been, prior to October of 1917, the Imperial Porcelain Factory. Located in Leningrad, it became, after the revolution, the State Porcelain Factory. In Imperial days, the factory's role had been to produce tableware and other porcelains for generations of Czars. After the revolution, new artisans used, in an appreciated irony, plates and other blanks previously marked with Imperial backstamps to convey messages for the proletarian masses using a variety of revolutionary icons and slogans. Of those involved in these endeavors at one time or another, the most notable was Vassily Kandinsky (1866–1944).

By 1910, his paintings were what we would now call "abstract"—so much so, in fact, that many of his canvasses seem incredibly progressive to and are definitely demanding of most viewers today. Even countless carefully chosen words cannot substitute for seeing what is being discussed here and so, to those with any interest in Noritake Art Deco, I urge that you find a copy of the book *Revolutionary Ceramics: Soviet Porcelain 1917–1927* by Nina Lobanov-Rostovsky (see *bibliography*). Even a cursory examination of the color photos in this excellent study will convince anyone that the themes of this movement are most assuredly expressed in post-1925 Noritake porcelains. A superb example—indeed, one that took my breath away when I first saw it—is the cream and sugar set on the cover of the book in your hands at this very moment. We may leave it to the experts to argue whether the works of Kandinsky himself inspired the Noritake Company designers who created the motif seen on this piece. They cannot plausibly deny, however, that the main character of the design is similar to Soviet Revolutionary ceramics for, as it happens, the cover of Lobanov-Rostovsky's book shows a plate with a motif-element almost exactly like the one that dominates the design of this amazing but appropriately utilitarian Noritake set.

The impact of Russia was felt far beyond the Soviet boundaries, however. In France, for example, the decorative arts of the inter-war years were shaped significantly by the Ballet Russes or, to be more precise, by the orientalist stage sets and costumes of Léon Bakst (c. 1867–1924). His work was also seen and admired in England, influencing Clarice Cliff (1899–1972) (among others) and in Austria where it influenced Josef Hoffman (1870–1956) and others associated with the now—and then—famous Bauhaus school, first at Weimar and then at Dessau. Although this school was active for only a few years (1919–1933), its impact was immense, especially on what we think of today as "modern"—i.e., "International Style"—architecture, furniture and allied design endeavors.

The Bauhaus was also influenced significantly by artistic ideas and associated conceptual developments that occurred in late nineteenth century Scotland—a trend known today as the "Arts and Crafts Movement." Much like the Italian Futurists (who, as previously noted, held center stage later—in the first decade or so of the twentieth century), leaders of the Arts and Crafts Movement, such as William Morris (1834–1896), wrote thoughtfully and extensively about their aims as artists. Unlike the Futurists, however, Morris and his associates as well as philosophical counterparts elsewhere, including Frank Lloyd Wright (1867–1959) eventually, were appalled by industrialism, especially as it was known during the mid-nineteenth century, especially but by no means exclusively in Great Britain. In response, they worked to establish guild-like craft workshops that designed and produced high quality, well functioning, moderately priced, serviceable goods—typically with minimal decorative detail. The well-known Morris chair is perhaps the quintessential example of such a product. It was built at the very successful furniture factory Morris established in 1861.

Disparate artistic developments such as these (and there were at least half a dozen others) neither were at the time nor are they now seen, collectively, as Art Deco. There is general agreement, however, that these are among the more significant lines of artistic development out of which what we now refer to as Art Deco, in its inclusive sense, coalesced by the mid-1920s. We must write (and say) "in its inclusive sense" because, for good or ill, the term "Art Deco" now includes a variety of distinct stylistic trends that, in the 1920s and after, were often at odds with each other (e.g., French Art Deco versus "modernism"). We must write (and say) "what we now refer to as Art Deco" because the term "Art Deco" itself was not coined until 1966. In that year, the Musée des Art Decoratifs held an exhibition in Paris that focused retrospectively on the dramatic developments in the decorative arts that originally had been showcased in Paris 70 years before at the *Exposition Internationale des Arts Décoratifs et Industriels Moderns*. The name of the 1966 show—*Art Deco/Bauhaus/Stijl/Espirit Nouveau*—was just as imposing. Again, for good or ill, it was soon shortened to "Art Deco" in most accounts of it.

The 1925 Paris Exposition, as I shall refer to it, was both huge and a huge success. Located in the center of the city, there were many very large venues for exhibits from numerous countries. Visitors came to see examples of "modern design"—the theme that had been announced in advance to all potential exhibitors, of which there were many, since the 1925 Exposition was actually an event first scheduled for 1912. And see it they did! It ran for over six months (from April through October) and, according to Garth Clark's "Introduction" (p.19) to Karen McCready's *Art Deco and Modernist Ceramics* (an *essential* work for any serious collector of Art Deco ceramics, including Noritake) the Exposition drew over 28 million visitors. By all accounts, the overall quality of the items on display, which ranged from individual vases to entire buildings, was little short of breathtaking, and the range of styles was, to put it mildly, tremendous.

Ironically, it has been suggested by several experts (e.g., Clark in McCready, 1995) that it is incorrect to think of the 1925 Paris Exposition as the *beginning* of Art Deco. Rather, at least according to this view, it was the *culmination* of a series of artistic and philosophical developments, the outlines of which were sketched above. This is not to say that those attending the Exposition saw the displays and said, in effect, "well that *was* nice" and went on to develop other decorative forms and modalities. Rather, the Exposition was, as it were, the apogee or "High Noon" of the history of Art Deco.

This claim is not even remotely a suggestion that the movement(s) declined in popularity after 1925. Obviously, just the opposite is the case. Within months of the start of the show, versions of the ideas that had been given concrete expression at the Exposition—artistic endeavors initially launched in widely separate locations 25 years before—were being seen in all the more cosmopolitan decorated environments of Europe and America, as well as in some of the major cities of Asia (e.g., Shanghai). Within ten years or so, there were traces of Paris 1925 in almost every town one happened to be in. Many of those traces can still be found if one looks—at everything from the graphic embellishments of high school yearbooks and public memorials to decorative details on elevator doors and theater exit lights.

For some things, it may well be that "nothing succeeds like success." For art styles, however, it may be that "nothing fails like too much success." Or, to put it another way, if everyone is doing it, it cannot be modern and, not long after The Paris Exposition of 1925, *everyone* was doing it, including the Noritake Company. After 1925, according to this view, Art Deco as a style (or styles) went from being "cutting edge" to cliché or, to put it even more bluntly, it went from Paris to Peoria. In short, when the decorative ideas shown to a fascinated world in 1925 were copied, modified and diffused into and onto everything from playing cards to skyscrapers, then, according to the experts who hold this view, it was debased.

Thoughts on the Elements of a Style

Given all this talk of the diversity of the styles on display in Paris in 1925 and of its subsequent and widespread popularity (and/or vulgarization), one may well ask whether there could possibly have been *any* common threads to Art Deco? To answer this, I believe one must first consider another much more difficult to answer question: *Why* did Art Deco happen? In general and judging by the relevant publications I have examined (as well as conversations I have had with art historians), this question seems to be given one of two kinds of answers: (1) the fairly vague and (2) the very vague. By contrast, I opt for a spot much further out on what might be a rather thin limb and assert the following.

Nearly all Art Deco works contain stylistic elements and/or have other qualities that clearly are expressions of the (often ambivalent) response of artists to the two most significant socioeconomic developments of the early twentieth century. The first of these is modern industrialism, which I take to be starkly different from, on the one hand, early or pre-modern forms of industrialism and, on the other, late or postmodern forms. The second development is modern internationalism. In its most basic sense, this refers to the emergence, for the first time, of a true world system, at the sociocultural and economic levels. Obviously, an early form of this was achieved in the nineteenth century as Europe colonized much of the so-called third world. The effort to gear up for and then to fight the War to End All Wars, however, brought this process to what turns out to have been only an early pinnacle (of sorts). Indeed, much like the post-1925 vulgarization of Art Deco, there were signs, by the mid-1920s, of the impending demise of European colonialism, in its nineteenth century form. These two factors do not tell the whole story, however. To be complete, this model must also take into account how these two factors were themselves shaped by 1920s post-war euphoria—a point to which we return shortly.

My first claim—that Art Deco motifs are in part a response to modern industrialism—has undoubtedly been noted before, but never more eloquently than by S. Gross in a captionless drawing in the *New Yorker* (February 6, 1989, p. 59). It is a factory scene, dominated by two *huge* gear wheels. On the sill of a nearby window, there is a small potted plant. It has a single bloom. In shape, the bloom looks just like one of the gears. The message: not only the arts and the rest of culture, but everything, including nature itself, has been and continues to be transformed by machines.

Art Deco artists and designers were acutely aware of this, and there are many examples. Here, we begin by looking at the decoration on two Noritake bowls shown in photo 2.1 (two are shown to demonstrate, once again, that most fancy line Noritake items were indeed completely hand painted). Obviously, one of the flowers in each of these small (2.0"h x 6.63"w x 5.75"d) bowls is quite gear-like, just like the flower in Gross's drawing, which just as obviously is quite like the gears in the huge piece of machinery that dominates the scene. Similarly, according to the view being put forward here, such machines loomed at least as large in the period between, say the 1890s and the 1920s, not only in mundane work-a-day life but also in the minds of many of our most gifted artists.

With this example in mind, notice how some of the same design features of the large drill chuck shown in photo 2.2 are found on (a) the Sunbeam iced tea maker shown in photo (2.3, on p. 13), (b) the Noritake bowls shown in photo B.224 and B.254 and (c) the Chrysler Building (for most, a photo is not required but, if you have my first Noritake book handy, see the model of it shown in photo 2.15, p.15).

Are not these diverse items kindred "souls," in terms of some of their more prominent design elements (e.g., the use of black lines, black triangles and shiny surfaces)? More importantly, ask yourself this admittedly somewhat absurd yet still useful question: could the appearance of the drill chuck have been influenced by the motif on the Noritake bowl or by the overall appearance of the Sunbeam tea pot, or would it have been, if anything, the other way around?

This is, obviously, something of a trick question, since all of these items were almost certainly designed independently of each other. But, if forced to choose, it seems fairly

2.2 Drill chuck.
3.9"h x 2.5"w.

clear that the motif on a Noritake bowl would never have any influence on the shape and appearance of something like a drill chuck. Drill chucks have the appearance they do because of their function—i.e., and expressed using an aphorism, "form follows function." This principle was, in fact, strongly endorsed by many "modernist" architects, designers and artisans in the 1920s and is still. What is fascinating is the extent to which this principle was extended into areas that did not so obviously require it.

For example, note how the *surface* of so many Art Deco objects have a smooth, sleek, efficient, streamlined look, Noritake lusterware eminent among them. Why is this? Some have suggested that this was one way for artists to reject Art Nouveau styles, thus giving their works a distinctive look. I find this explanation unsatisfying. In the first place, I find compelling the case made by several scholars that Art Deco was *not* a style created in an effort to supplant Art Nouveau (for a good and brief account, see Duncan, 1988). Although easy to do, it is a mistake to assume that a style that follows another one chronologically is simply the earlier style's antithesis. Art Nouveau is better understood, according to this view, as one of many artistic approaches that fed into what became Art Deco. In addition, I happen to be one of those who continues to be impressed by the explanatory salience or formative power of the various technological and economic factors that predominate in a community. As I read the record, anyway, it appears that people *must* and do (again, for reasons that will not be reviewed here) respond to such factors, both socially and aesthetically.

I turn now, briefly, to the second of my two claims, the one regarding what I have referred to as "internationalism." People in all times and places have been fascinated by what they think of as exotic peoples. This includes being intrigued by all that goes into making them so—their clothes, foods, dances, houses, arts, philosophical outlook, and all the rest. This fascination usually takes one of two forms: positive or negative. The negative forms vary in their details but always entail beliefs about the *inferiority* of the exotic others. Sadly, this response, along with various associated forms of violence, has almost certainly been the

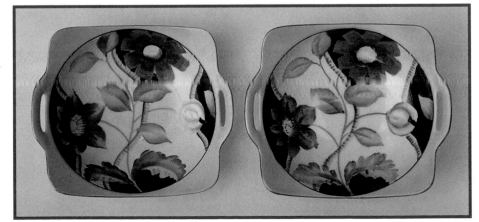

2.1 Bowls. 2.0"h x 6.63"w x 5.75"d. Backstamp: 27.1.

more common one in human history, both recent and more distant. The positive forms involve the *admiration* and, even, the *idealization* of exotic others. This too can take many forms but always will involve some degree of emulation—e.g., the adopting of such customary aspects of admired peoples as their clothes, religious beliefs, food and art.

In the nineteenth century, the peoples of the world considered exotic from the standpoint of Europe and America were seen variously, to be sure, but in general they were seen as being inferior and as inferior beings. In the two decades before the 1920s, however, many artists and others (including anthropologists) began to question this viewpoint profoundly. By way of example from the arts, we may recall the famous case of the *very* positive response of Georges Braque (1882–1963), Pablo Picasso (1881–1973), and others to African masks and other tribal art displayed in Paris prior to World War I. Although admittedly an overstatement, the significance of this influence is shown by the often-heard suggestion that Cubism owes as much to artists from West and Central Africa whose names we do not know as it does to Braque and Picasso.

A closely related artistic cum political development, albeit less well-known today, also occurred in Paris at about the same time (the 1920s). It was led by Léopold Sédar Senghor (b. 1906), a gifted writer and, from 1960-1980, the President of Senegal (in West Africa). One of the movement's central concepts was "negritude"—an intensely positive stance regarding Africans and African culture that, within a few decades, would evolve into the "black is beautiful" movement in America. In America, similar views were being expressed about exotic cultures generally by cultural anthropologists. Especially noteworthy in this regard are the scholarly writings of Ruth Fulton Benedict (1887–1948) and particularly her book *Patterns of Culture,* in which she vigorously made the case for cultural relativism and the dignity and worth of *all* cultures. Although not published until after the 1920s (in 1934), its intellectual foundation was laid at least 30 years before that. Her thoughts about other peoples and cultures, it is important to emphasize, were not obscure ideas known to only a few ivory-tower-bound academics. Rather, they clearly touched a theme of interest to many, at least in America, as may be judged by the fact that her book was read approvingly by millions. Among them were many thousands who could use newly built (post World War I) railroads to travel easily from New York to one of the places discussed extensively in Benedict's now classic work—the then comparatively exotic American Southwest. Not coincidentally, many 1920s Art Deco motifs convey a strong flavor of the decorative arts of this distinctive cultural area. There are several striking Noritake examples shown in this book, among them being the bowls shown in B.216 and B.293 as well as the vase shown in V.247.

These two factors—modern industrialism and internationalism—were expressed distinctively and in different proportions from one place and time to another. Sometimes, these themes would be equally in evidence; at other times, the one or the other of them would clearly predominate.

Frequently but by no means always, these aspects of Art Deco motifs were also shaped by the sheer enthusiasm and optimism brought on by the ending of World War I and economic recovery in America and in much of Europe. It made it possible, once again, for opulence to be a vital part of the sensibility of the times. Nowhere was this more evident than in the opulent, gaudy, rich, intense, gilded and lavish displays by French designers at the 1925 Paris Exposition. So distinctive were these efforts that, retrospectively, their viewpoint regarding decoration would be referred to as French Art Deco to distinguish it from the more streamlined, modernist efforts of designers elsewhere. This is appropriate, I think, because the French approach was almost unique. Much of the rest of what we now think of as Art Deco was, by comparison, so much more severe.

Many Noritake porcelains exemplify this French tone, I think. In this book, the best example is almost certainly the jam set shown on the cover and below in Chapter C (C.133). The late Howard Kottler, who liked to give names to the designs on Noritake, called this motif "Jewels." It is a term that fits not only the particulars of the design but also the character of French Art Deco (though this does not mean it was Kottler's motive for selecting the name). Opulence also shows up in two other types of motifs on Noritake porcelains: certain of the floral designs and, perhaps more obviously, in pieces displaying examples of 1920s high fashion which, without a doubt, were heavily influenced by French sensibilities. Thus, almost all so-called Noritake "lady pieces" are of interest to Art Deco collectors, whether they specialize in Noritake or not. Such lady pieces include more than those that display obvious 1920s fashion ingredients (cloche hats, long strings of beads, bias-cut, body clinging fabrics). Included as well are fashion elements (turbans, Chinese high-collar coats) and settings that can only be described, from the European vantage point, as exotic (*not* "ethnic"—that would come later). Two *great* Noritake examples of the latter are the motifs (both fashion and setting) on the cake plates in P.137 and P.138.

These claims about fashion can be validated in many ways. For our purposes, a recent publication entitled *French Art Deco Fashions* will suffice (see *bibliography* for details). This book shows a selection of pochoir prints from *Art–Gout–Beauté* (Art–Style–Beauty), a French fabric manufacturer's periodical from the 1920s. The term "pochoir" refers to a type of stencil print developed in Paris at the end of the last century. This method for making multiple copies of prints was itself based on Japanese techniques long employed to decorate fabrics. The color reproductions of these prints are, of course, the heart of the book, but the soul of it is in the words. These words, which read almost like the diary entries of young fashion-conscious women, were apparently (it is never made explicitly clear, unfortunately) the text in the magazine. For the most part, they are pure fantasy and yet they well convey the sense of opulence and indulgence that was so characteristic of not only French high fashion but also of French Art Deco as a whole. Consider this one example (p.49):

Our hats, our dresses, our handbags, our stockings, our shoes, our gloves, all give way to this rite of metallic skin, gilded with gold or silver; they are found everywhere, in pieces of braid, in cloth cut on the bias, in rosettes, in tablecloths, in inlays, in ribbons, in fringes, in flowers, in petals; it is printed, carved, painted, hemstitched, embroidered, sequined, and pearlized. It is combined with feathers, fur, satin, velours, and crepes; for the evening as well as the morning, sporty or fashionable.

On and on it goes; page after page of musings about (using their words again) "what sudden and inexplicable whims style can suddenly have" (p.49). Sudden, perhaps; inexplicable perhaps not. Opulence comes in many forms. The form we associate with Art Deco is not at all the opulence of, say, the 1890s or that little era at the start of the century that ended in 1914. By the 1920s, amazing machines and admired exotics had worked their magic. Mind-jarring abstractions, jazzy angularity, hard geometry and curves suggestive of motion and power came to the foreground. Realism, symmetry, balance and curves suggestive of lush nature were either transformed and moved to the background or dropped altogether.

In terms of the decorative arts, we see, for example, exotic materials, sometimes clearly linked to machines (stainless steel, chrome) and at other times, expressive of nature transformed to machine-like polish (e.g., ebony, mother-of-pearl inlays). Machine-made colors, such as the metallic blues, greens, tans and oranges of Noritake luster, rather than those typically seen in nature, come to the foreground. The "pure" greens of grass and shrub give way to the "off" greens of mint. The orange of oranges gives way to the tan of tangerines. The blue of skies is replaced by the turquoise of rocks. Objects of nature—roses, trees, animals—are made to exhibit unnatural colors, sizes and shapes. We do not see prize examples of ordinary nature but ordinary examples of nature at its most surprising—

2.3 Sunbeam Iced Tea Maker. 10.75"h x 6.0"w.

exotic animals, weird plants, unrealistic colors, impossible sizes. Although virtually all of nature unavoidably shows the effects of human activity, the landscapes of the 1920s, as seen on Noritake porcelains for example, depict nature transformed by *modern* human endeavors. Post-1925 Noritake Art Deco landscapes do not show the nature of rural sentimentality designed to mesmerize; this nature has an urban sensibility designed to energize.

As if to keep pace with the new speed of life (and the life of speed) of the 1920s, Art Deco motifs frequently seem designed more to *suggest* ideas than to *present* them fully developed. Abstraction and stylization predominate; details and thoroughgoing realism are no longer possible. Motion is shown, not with the static depiction of an airplane but, rather and more effectively, with the swish of few well placed speed stripes. Power is shown, ironically, not by depicting giant elephants or burly bears but, rather, by graceful gazelles known for their leaping prowess and, most of all, speed. Even flowers were given great power—not by depicting them in all their natural beauty and exquisite detail but, rather, by giving them unnatural shapes and colors. Sometimes it is hard to say precisely how the message of power comes though. Perhaps one senses the tremendous effort that would be required, in nature, to create such components and then to hold them in place.

In summary, Art Deco is a complex of diverse decorative arts viewpoints that coalesced in the 1925 Paris Exposition. As a cutting edge viewpoint, its decline can be said to have begun at that point. As a popular decorative arts movement—certainly the most popular one of the twentieth century—it can be said to have begun to blossom at that point. It was not simply the antithesis of the realism and naturalness of Art Nouveau, but it is correct to say that it was the opposite of Art Nouveau in many ways. The contrast is more than the domestic and natural versus the international and machine-made, but not much more. It is the power of nature versus the nature of power, mainline versus streamlined, harmonious versus jarring, the familiar versus the strange, symmetry versus asymmetry, rural versus urban, provincial versus cosmopolitan, the waltz versus the Charleston, Sousa marches versus New Orleans jazz, still life versus Cubism, the holistic versus the fractured. In a few words, it is the traditional versus the modern, just as the organizers of the 1925 Paris Exposition wanted it to be.

Neither the previous paragraph nor this entire chapter says all that could or should be said about Art Deco in general or about Noritake Art Deco porcelains in particular. I never thought it would be possible, here, to be definitive; rather, my more modest and realistic goal has been merely to suggest and point to major themes. Details and examples are needed, to be sure. With but a few exceptions, they have not been provided in this chapter. Rather, they are offered in the introductions to the individual chapters of Part Two (particularly chapters A, B, C, P and V). There, I say a few additional things about Art Deco generally and a lot about Art Deco Noritake in particular. In each case, I do so while citing numerous examples from the materials within a given chapter.

Chapter 3

Noritake Backstamps:
An Overview and Update

The very fact that you have read even this far into this chapter may well be sufficient for you to lay claim to membership in a fairly small and (if I may say so) elite group. What I am told, by more than a few Noritake collectors and dealers, is that they are not interested in what they see as the hopelessly arcane, excessively detailed, unnecessarily fussy subject of Noritake backstamps. Well you know what? I sympathize with such viewpoints. Who in their right mind should *want* to spend a lot of time trying to master anything that could be described like that! Rather, in this chapter the whole subject is treated briefly and in a completely non-technical manner, using a question-and-answer format. It is, in other words, as "user-friendly" as can be.

What topics are discussed in this chapter?

As you read on, you will be given some important new information about Noritake backstamps and a *few* key facts that you really ought to know about the meaning of the backstamp numbers. You will also see a new double backstamp oddity, one that complements the double backstamped piece shown in my first Noritake book. Finally, you will come to Table 3.1. This table is a more accurate and up-to-date version of the Table 3.1 that was in my first Noritake book. In it, you will find: (1) a listing of the backstamp numbers used in this and my previous Noritake book coordinated with (2) the backstamp numbers used in three other books on Noritake collectibles, augmented by (3) updated information on the dates these backstamps were registered, *according to the Noritake Company itself*. For this feature of the table, which is of great importance to both collectors and dealers, we all owe a huge debt of gratitude to Mr. Keishi ("Casey") Suzuki, of the Noritake Company. It was he who led the effort to gather the data on Noritake Company backstamps and then to publish a truly wonderful pamphlet on the subject. In conjunction with Table 3.1, there is an expanded and easy-to-use color photo display of the Noritake backstamps found on pieces in this and my previous Noritake book.

Are the backstamps shown in this book and/or discussed in Table 3.1 the only ones known to have been used by the Noritake Company?

No. The 55 backstamps shown with Table 3.1 below are merely the ones found on pieces shown in this and/or in my previous book on Noritake collectibles. There are literally hundreds of Noritake backstamps, not even counting those that appear on dinnerware with specific pattern names. The Noritake Company pamphlet mentioned above, for example, shows over 300 backstamps.

What is a Noritake backstamp?

There are two ways to answer this question. As posed, and because the question was not "What is a Noritake *Company* backstamp?" We may say, first, that a "Noritake backstamp" is essentially any backstamp that one finds on the pieces collected by "Noritake collectors." Those are the only backstamps relevant for a book having the scope and purposes of one such as this. I do not show or discuss *all* "Noritake backstamps," however. Instead, I limit the backstamps shown in this book to those that appear on pieces in the book (or in my previous one). Other Noritake backstamps relevant to collectors besides those shown here are known and, when needed, will be shown, in color, in any future books I do on this subject.

The second answer to this question shifts our direction significantly to a consideration of whether *all* the words, letters and marks that one may find on the bottom of Noritake porcelains are in fact part of the "backstamp." This comes up because, on some Noritake pieces, there are words near a generally recognized backstamp, put there by the Noritake Company, which give information such as the number of pieces made, the occasions for which the pieces were made or for whom they were made. In this book, such words and marks usually are not part of the "backstamp" in the narrow or "proper" sense. For example look at photo B.310A (p.76). It shows the bottom of the piece shown in photo B.310. We may ask whether all of the words and other things you see in the photograph are part of some sort of *specific* backstamp that ought to have its own backstamp number. My answer is "no." Words like "Hotel McAlpin" or a date such as "New Year's Eve 1931" are not part of the backstamp in the narrow sense. On this piece, the "backstamp" is the familiar "M-in-Wreath" symbol on the right. Thus, in the photo caption of the piece in Chapter B, it states that the backstamp is 25.0 (which is how this particular version of the "M-in-Wreath" backstamp has been designated in this book). In the captions in Part Two, however, important or interesting supplementary words often will be noted, usually within parentheses after the backstamp number or in an accompanying photo or, in some cases, both.

Is the "Cherry Blossom" backstamp a genuine Noritake backstamp?

In contrast to the situation in 1997, when my first Noritake book was published, we may now answer this question with a resounding "yes." We now know for sure (for reasons noted below) that the Cherry Blossom backstamp (see photos 3.16, 3.17 and 3.18, below, p.20) *is* a genuine Noritake backstamp. For years, however, collectors and dealers alike had doubts about whether pieces with this backstamp had truly been made by the Noritake Company. There were two good reasons for this doubt. First, this backstamp does not have the word "Noritake" in it, while virtually all others used during the 1920s did (the 1920s time period is important here since, stylistically, the pieces with Cherry Blossom backstamps were so obviously from this era). Second, the admittedly abbreviated Company-provided list of Noritake backstamps available prior to 1997 did not mention it. It was impossible, therefore, to be completely confident about this backstamp at the time I was working on my first Noritake book.

Given the doubts *and* the high interest in the subject among collectors, I carefully reviewed three kinds of evidence that seemed relevant, or at least potentially so, for deciding whether the Cherry Blossom backstamp was a true Noritake backstamp. First, I examined the published views of two expert Noritake collectors who had said the backstamp was indeed a Noritake mark. Second, I noted that some items with a known Noritake backstamp matched exactly a piece with a Cherry Blossom backstamp and showed an example. Third, I provided photographic evidence that, sometimes, a piece had *both* a known Noritake backstamp *and* a Cherry Blossom backstamp (see photo 3.1, below).

3.1 **Backstamps 16.0 and 19.1** on one piece (as shown in Book I).

Interestingly, another piece with a double backstamp has turned up in the meantime. In this instance, however, the Cherry Blossom backstamp is accompanied by the classic M-in-Wreath backstamp, but they are superimposed rather than side by side (see photo 3.2, below).

3.2. **Backstamps 19.0 and 27.0,** superimposed on one piece.

In light of all these factors, I concluded, confidently but still with an awareness that I might be wrong, that pieces with such backstamps had been made by the Noritake Company and should therefore be included in my book. In spite of what seemed like almost overwhelming evidence, my tentativeness on this matter seemed only prudent since, at the time I was writing, I knew of no official statement about this backstamp by the Noritake Company itself. Now, however, the company has provided one. This statement occurs in a pamphlet published in English by the Noritake Company in May 1997—at the same time as my first Noritake book was being printed (see *Noritake: History of the Materials Development and Chronology of the Backstamps*). When I finally received a copy of the pamphlet, I learned that it had been first published in September of 1995, in Japanese. I, however, had neither seen it nor been informed as to its contents until after my book came out.

According to the Noritake Company, the Cherry Blossom backstamp (number 33 in the Noritake Company list) was registered in 1924. This backstamp (it is also noted on page 12 of the Noritake Company pamphlet) was used on pieces "which failed to reach the quality level of Noritake in terms of body and painting." This extremely important comment itself requires comment. As a statement made by the Noritake Company about the varying quality of decorations on its own pieces, this is assuredly of general interest to serious collectors and dealers. Far more important, however, such a statement greatly increases the likelihood that collectors and dealers will henceforth presume more-or-less automatically that any piece with a Cherry Blossom backstamp must necessarily be inferior to Noritake marked pieces. Similarly, since quality is closely linked to value (and price), many can also be expected to presume that a piece with a Cherry Blossom backstamp should automatically be lower in price than other similar pieces with Noritake backstamps. In many cases, these views may well be correct. The danger comes if this reasoning is accepted too readily or automatically. Collectors and dealers should *not* use this comment by the Noritake Company mindlessly; instead, we all need to evaluate items with a Cherry Blossom backstamp on a "case-by-case" basis—something that *should* be done, of course, with *all* Noritake porcelains, no matter what the backstamp.

What do the backstamp numbers (e.g., in the captions) mean?

This question is answered thoroughly in my first book on Noritake collectibles. In the Chapter 3 of that book, I explained, carefully and in some detail, how I picked the numbers that were used to identify backstamps (e.g., in captions). I still think that was a useful exercise and, for those interested in my thinking on the subject, I still recommend giving that chapter at least a quick read. Even so, just as one does not need to know how a watch works in order to tell what time it is by looking at one, readers can make perfectly good use of the caption information in this book without knowing *why* I use the numbers I do to designate the many and varied backstamps found on the pieces shown in this book.

Instead, one can treat the numbers as though there were merely simple labels that may be used to locate backstamps that are displayed, in numerical order, along with Table 3.1 (below). Thus, anyone who is curious about what the backstamp on a given piece looks like need only note its number and then look it up there (pp. 20-22).

Why do the backstamp numbers in
this book have decimal values (e.g., 27.1)?

As you will see soon enough, if you are not familiar with this fact already, all the backstamp numbers in this book consist of numerals placed to the right *and* left of a decimal point. In the question, the example was 27.1 but, in general form, the numbers can look like this: ##.# or this: ##.## or, sometimes, like this: ##.###. Even bigger numbers are possible. (For a more complete explantion of my numbering system, please see my first book, *Noritake Collectibles A to Z*.)

There is, however, an important advantage in learning just two simple things about *one* part of the backstamp number—namely, the part to the *right* of the decimal. This part of the number identifies the color or colors of a backstamp, and, for various reasons, this seems to be something that many collectors and dealers are quite interested in. This being so, let me tell you the two things you need to know in order to "read" what the numerals to the right of the decimal say with regard to color.

The first thing to know is that the *order* of the numerals to the right of the decimal has no meaning. A sequence like 15 would convey the same information as 51. (For the sake of simplicity and standardization, however, I decided I would always put the numerals in order from lowest to highest moving from left to right.)

The second thing you need to know is that each numeral to the right of the decimal designates a color (or in some cases, several differently named shades of a color). The most common backstamp colors on Noritake wares of the sort shown in this book are green and red. Because of this, I began the list of numerals linked to color with these two colors.

The entire list, including the decimal point, is shown below:

    .0 = green
    .1 = red (or maroon)
    .2 = blue
    .3 = magenta (similar to but not the same as red or maroon)
    .4 = teal (similar to but not the same as blue)
    .5 = black
    .6 = yellow (including mustard and similar shades but not gold)
    .7 = gold
    .8 = silver (including metallic—e.g., backstamps embossed in metal)
    .9 = tan, brown, beige and other similar shades.

Thus, in the case of the example given in the question (it was 27.1), the 1 to the right of the decimal means the backstamp is red (entirely). If it had been 27.15, then it would mean that it was red *and* black.

I don't know of anyone who has memorized this entire list. I know I haven't! It simply is not worth the effort when it is so easy to look up. Even so, readers will soon discover that the first three numerals above (.0, .1, .2) occur quite frequently, so you may find it helpful to learn what these numbers mean with reference to color.

Why should collectors bother with details
about the backstamps anyway? Aren't we really interested
in the other side of Noritake porcelains we collect?

There are basically two reasons to pay any attention at all to backstamps. For most dealers and collectors, the primary issue (phrased as a question) is about origins: did the Noritake Company really make the piece I am looking at? The secondary one (also expressed as a question) is about chronology: when was the piece made? As it happens, backstamps are a lot more helpful regarding origins than chronology. Thus, the user of this book who has or is thinking of acquiring a piece of porcelain with a backstamp exactly like those shown in Table 3.1 (including the photos) can reasonably be sure of two things: (1) that it was made by the Noritake Company and, therefore, (2) that it is of interest to (i.e., it probably is collected by) at least some of those who define themselves as "Noritake collectors."

If the piece in question has a backstamp that is *similar* to one shown here, it *might* have been made by the Noritake Company. The supposition is that the piece happens to have a backstamp that is just a variant of one shown here.

However, there *are* backstamps similar to those shown here that *are not* Noritake Company backstamps. In this case, one cannot conclude the similar backstamp is a variant. The advice of an expert should be sought.

Matters of chronology, however, are far more problematic than issues of manufacture. There are three main reasons for this. First, although registration dates for quite a few of the backstamps are provided here, these provide little more than rough estimates of dates, since it is known that some backstamps were not used as soon as they were registered. This appears to have been the case for the important No. 27. backstamp, for example. This situation is compounded by a second issue: some backstamps appear to have been used for a time, then not used and then changed just slightly and used later. If one does not notice such things as, for example, very small differences in the size and shape of certain letters or the presence or absence of certain very tiny design elements such as dots, one can draw erroneous conclusions about which backstamp one is actually looking at and, therefore, what the age of the piece is. Many of these points arise with the various forms of the widely seen Komaru backstamps (No.16. and variants), for example. Finally, some backstamps apparently were used for several decades or more. Again, this point is illustrated by Komaru backstamps. Given all of this, collectors and dealers are strongly advised (and here we return to the sentiments expressed in the second of the two questions above which launched me into these comments) to pay at least as much attention to matters of decorative style as to backstamp registration dates when attempting to determine the age of a piece of Noritake porcelain.

Is this all we need to know about the backstamps shown in this book?

Yes, although there are many other things that could be said and, even, a few that I am very tempted to discuss (for examples, see Chapter 3 of *Noritake Collectibles, A to Z*). For most readers and for general purposes, however, what has been said here is about all one needs to know about the backstamps shown in this book. This being the case, I invite you to examine Table 3.1 (pp.18-22).

What information is displayed Table in 3.1?

This table displays important information, in summary form, about the backstamps commonly seen on the porcelains that are the subject of this book. This table is *not* nor was it ever intended to be a complete compendium of Noritake Company backstamps. Neither is it a record of all backstamps of possible interest to Noritake collectors. With one or two exceptions, the backstamps described in this table appear on an item shown in this or my previous Noritake book. The backstamp numbers used in this book are in the column headed "DHS #s."

Users of this table can easily make quite good use of the information provided here, even if they have not read Chapter 3 of my first book They may be puzzled, however, to see that some numbers appear to have been skipped (the first backstamp number in the table, for example, is .07). The unused numbers were not "skipped" accidentally but, rather, are simply not currently assigned. This happens because the backstamp numbering system used in this book is more than an enumeration of backstamps (a feature of the numbering system in use here that is not discussed in this book; although it is discussed in my first book). In the future, some of the currently unused numbers may well be used; some may never be used.

What do the column headings mean?

The table below has eight columns:

Column 1, on the far left (DHS #s), shows, with two exceptions, the numerals to the left of the decimal, which designate the "specific kinds" of Noritake backstamp relevant to this book. The exceptions are two backstamps designated entirely by letters—either J or MIJ, standing respectively for "Japan" and "Made in Japan." Usually, these words occur on pieces, particularly from the 1920s, which were parts of larger sets or which were too small to permit the application of the full backstamp (or both). In such cases, the Noritake Company simply marked a piece with the words "Japan" or "Made in Japan." Because those words are also found on many non-Noritake Company porcelains, collectors and dealers should make sure that the words in these two backstamps match, in color, size and other characteristics, these same words as found on full Noritake backstamps (and especially backstamp No. 27.). Sometimes, in Column 1, the numerals to the right of the decimal also will be given.

Column 2 (Description) states, as briefly as possible using words, what the defining features of the backstamps are. This is a simplified guide only. All the backstamps described here are shown in photos at the end of this table. Users should certainly consult those photos. Also in this column, when appropriate, certain features that one may notice but which are *not* "defining features" will be mentioned. Unless stated otherwise, all of these backstamps contain the word "Noritake" and none have the word "Nippon," except when it is part of the phrase "Nippon Toki Kaisha," which means, in essence, "Japanese Ceramics Company."

Column 3 (Year) gives, according to Noritake Company information (see *bibliography* for further information about their backstamp pamphlet), the year of *registration* of the backstamp or the year when *production* of pieces bearing the backstamp started. These years, therefore, give only a very rough estimate of the age of a piece with a given backstamp.

Column 4 (D or E) indicates, again using information from the Noritake Company, whether a backstamp was used for goods *exported* (E) from Japan or sold *domestically* (D)—i.e., within Japan. Columns 5-8 (A&R #s, LAD #s, NCO #s, JVP #s) provide a cross-reference to the numbers used for these backstamps (or their nearest equivalents) by, respectively, Alden and Richardson, Lou Ann Donahue, the Noritake Company and Joan Van Patten (see bibliography).

Table 3.1: An Updated List of Noritake Backstamps

DHS #s	DEFINING FEATURES OF SPECIFIC KINDS OF NORITAKE BACKSTAMPS	YEAR	D/ E	A&R #s	LAD #s	NCO #s	JVP #s
J.	The word "Japan," in colors and general appearance as found on backstamp 27	1918?	E	none	none	none	none
MIJ.	The words "Made in Japan," like those found on backstamp 27	1918?	E	none	none	none	none
07.0	RC + Balance symbol + Nippon Toki Kaisha + Chinese/Japanese characters in green; sometimes with a design number	1912	D	none	none	20	7
07.3	RC + Balance symbol + Nippon Toki Kaisha + Chinese/Japanese characters in magenta (found on especially fine, highly decorated sets, often with extensive gold)	1912	D	none	none	20	7
07.7	RC + Balance symbol + Nippon Toki Kaisha + Chinese/Japanese characters in gold	1912	D	none	none	20	7
14.	Komaru symbol + Made in Japan + Design Patent Applied For	?	E?	none	none	10? 120?	17
15.01	Komaru symbol + Made in Japan (in green) + Chinese/Japanese characters (in red) (whether or not there is a design number which, in captions, is given within parentheses with backstamp number)	?	E?	MM-9A	none	10? 120?	none
16.0	Komaru symbol + Made in Japan in green (but no Chinese/Japanese characters)	1908 and 1949	E	none	11	10 and 120	16
16.1	Komaru symbol + Made in Japan in red (but no Chinese/Japanese characters)	1908 and 1949	E	none	11	10 and 120	16
16.4	Komaru symbol + Made in Japan in teal (but no Chinese/Japanese characters); has an accent on the "e" in Noritake, a flat-topped letter "r" & thick central element	1908	E	MM-9	11	9	16
18.	Large letter M inside a thin 5-lobed "cherry blossom" + Made in Japan + the word "Noritake"	1925	E	MM-20	none	34	none
19.0	5-lobed "cherry blossom" with a center of radiating lines + Made in Japan or just Japan but without the word "Noritake"; in green; decorated by subcontractors	1924	E	MM-23 with no pattern name	none	33	none
19.1	5-lobed "cherry blossom" with a center of radiating lines + Made in Japan or just Japan but without the word "Noritake; in red; decorated by subcontractors	1924	E	MM-23 with no pattern name	none	33	none
19.2	5-lobed "cherry blossom" with a center of radiating lines + Made in Japan or just Japan but without the word "Noritake; in blue; decorated by subcontractors	1924	E	MM-23 with no pattern name	none	33	none
21.	Large letter M inside an abstract wreath + Japan	1935	E	MM-15	none	87	none
24.	M-in-Wreath + Japan (no "Handpainted" or "Made in")	1918	E	MM-18	none	29	52
25.	M-in-Wreath + Handpainted + Japan (no "Made in")	1918	E	MM-26	none	29	50
26.0	M-in-Wreath + Made in Japan (no "Handpainted") in green	1918	E	none	10	29	38
26.1	M-in-Wreath + Made in Japan (no "Handpainted") in red	1918	E	MM-22	10	29	38
27.0	M-in-Wreath + Handpainted + Made in Japan in green	1918	E	MM-19	9	29	27
27.1	M-in-Wreath + Handpainted + Made in Japan in red (decorated by Noritake Company subcontractors)	1918	E	MM-19A	9	29	27
27.2	M-in-Wreath + Handpainted + Made in Japan in blue (on some items for children)	1918	E	none	none	29	none
27.3	M-in-Wreath + Handpainted + Made in Japan in magenta (on fine, highly decorated sets often with extensive gold)	1918	E	A&M-19A	none	29	none

DHS #s	DEFINING FEATURES OF SPECIFIC KINDS OF NORITAKE BACKSTAMPS	YEAR	D/E	A&R #s	LAD #s	NCO #s	JVP #s
28.	M-in-Wreath + Made in Japan + Design Patent Applied For [ignores variations due to abbreviations whether it has the words "Handpainted" and "Made in" and/or to the presence of various pattern names, which, in captions, are added in parentheses after the backstamp number—e.g., 28.1 (Roseara)]	1918	E	MM-22B & C, plus MM-19B & G-L plus others	none	29	28 plus 36, 39, 41-48 and 98
29.	M-in-Wreath + Made in Japan + any Chinese/Japanese characters [ignores variations due to whether it says "Hand-painted" or "Made in" or to the particulars of pattern numbers which, in captions, are added in parentheses after the backstamp number —e.g., 29.1 (29812) —the Azalea pattern number is 19322]	1918	E	MM-19C & D-F	none	29	29 plus 30-35 37, 49 & 99
33.	Shield-and-Wreath-under-Crown	1935	E	none	none	86	none
38.1	M-with-Banner-and-Crown + Handpainted + Japan (in maroon)	1940	E	like MM-42	none	107	79
39.	M-with-Banner-and-Crown + Japan (no "Handpainted")	1940?	E	MM-43	24?	107?	none
50.	Komaru symbol + Nippon Toki Kaisha	1949	D	MM-50	27	119	90
54.	Komaru-in-Wreath + Made in Japan	1933	E	none	none	61	none
55.	Komaru-in-Wreath + Bone China + Nippon Toki Kaisha (does not have the word "Noritake")	1940	D	none	21	105	80
56.15	Komaru-in-Wreath + Bone China + Nippon Toki Kaisha (in black) + Made in Japan (in red) (does not have the word "Noritake")	1940?	E?	none	none	none	none
64.019	Bowl-in-Wreath + Bone China + Nippon Toki (no "Kaisha"; green, red & brown)	1946?	D	none	none	109?	none
65.019	Bowl-in-Wreath + Bone China + Nippon Toki Kaisha + Japan (green, red & brown)	1946?	D?	none	29	109?	85?
65.5	Bowl-in-Wreath + Bone China + Nippon Toki Kaisha + Japan (in black)	1946?	D?	none	none	109?	85
66.57	Bowl-in-Wreath + Bone China + ® + Japan (in black and gold)	1980	E & D	none	57	231	86
67.019	Bowl-in-Wreath + Bone China + Nippon Toki Kaisha (no Japan or Made in Japan) (in green, red and brown)	1946	D	none	none	109	none
70.7	Noritake Bone China Japan (in gold script; ignores edition numbers and similar details; if info. is available will be noted in caption in parentheses after the backstamp number)	1950?	E	none	none	123?	none
71.7	Noritake (in script) + (in block letters; in gold) Bone China A Limited Edition (of some number) + Japan	1950?	E	none	none	123?	none
72.	N-in-Wreath-with-Bow + Bone China + ® + Japan	1986	D	none	none	261	none
74.	N-in-Wreath-with-Bow + ® + Japan (ignores variations due to two tiny dots in the wreath of some versions)	1968	E & D	none	none	154	94
76.	N-in-Wreath (no bow) + Nippon Toki Kaisha + Japan	1955	D	none	none	135	96
77.	N-in-Wreath (no bow) + Nippon Toki Kaisha (but no Japan)	1955?	D?	none	none	135?	none
78.	N-in-Wreath (no bow) + Studio Collection + Bone China + Japan	1976	D	none	none	207	none
86.	Noritake Legacy Philippines	1977	E	none	none	218	none

3.3 Backstamp MIJ.1

3.4 Backstamp 07.0

3.5 Backstamp 07.0 (46755)

3.6 Backstamp 07.3

3.7 Backstamp 07.7

3.8 Backstamp 14.0

3.9 Backstamp 14.0 (39539)

3.10 Backstamp 15.01

3.11 Backstamp 16.0

3.12 Backstamp 16.1

3.13 Backstamp 16.4

3.14 Backstamp 16.7

3.15 Backstamp 18.0

3.16 Backstamp 19.0

3.17 Backstamp 19.1

3.18 Backstamp 19.2

3.19 Backstamp 21.0

3.20 Backstamp 24.1

3.21 Backstamp 25.0

3.22 Backstamp 25.1

3.23 Backstamp 26.0

3.24 Backstamp 26.1

3.25 **Backstamp 26.8**

3.26 **Backstamp 27.0**

3.27 **Backstamp 27.1**

3.28 **Backstamp 27.2**

3.29 **Backstamp 27.3**

3.30 **Backstamp 28.1**

3.31 **Backstamp 28.1** (Roseara)

3.32 **Backstamp 29.1**

3.33 **Backstamp 29.1 (19322)**

3.34 **Backstamp 29.1 (29812)**

3.35 **Backstamp 29.7 (20056)**

3.36 **Backstamp 33.056**

3.37 **Backstamp 38.1**

3.38 **Backstamp 39.019**

3.39 **Backstamp 43.056**

3.40 **Backstamp 50.3**

3.41 **Backstamp 54.0**

3.42 **Backstamp 55.5**

3.43 **Backstamp 56.15**

3.44 **Backstamp 64.019**

3.45 **Backstamp 65.019**

3.46 **Backstamp 65.5**

3.47 **Backstamp 66.57**

3.48 **Backstamp 67.019**

3.49 **Backstamp 70.7** (Fifth Edition)

3.50 **Backstamp 70.7** (Mother's Day 1976, Third Edition, One of 2,800)

3.51 **Backstamp 71.7** (A Limited Edition of 10,000)

3.52 **Backstamp 72.7**

3.53 **Backstamp 74.5**

3.54 **Backstamp 76.3**

3.55 **Backstamp 77.3**

3.56 **Backstamp 78.9**

3.57 **Backstamp 86.5**

Part Two
Introduction

Part Two is, as it were, the meat and potatoes portion of this book. It is where most users of the book will spend most of their time. Since the most delicious things in the book are to be found here, some may prefer to think of Part Two as the dessert portion (in contrast to the lima beans of Chapter 3). Whichever it is, you can be sure of one thing: because of the way Part Two is organized, you can easily and effectively use it, even if you do not read past the end of this sentence. If you do read on, though, the three most important keys to the organization of Part Two will be explained briefly: (1) how and why the photographic materials were clustered into letter-designated chapters, (2) how, in general, the photos are laid out on the pages, and (3) how the photo captions are structured.

Chapter Organization

The chapters in Part Two are designated, as you may have noticed already, by letters rather than the more usual numbers. These chapters are arranged alphabetically with reference to the letter used to designate a chapter. This was done to make the book easy to use as a reference tool. The chapter-designating letters have mnemonic value. In other words, the letters are meant to help users quickly figure out and then easily remember where things of interest to them are likely to be in this book. For example, if you happened to be interested in seeing photos of Noritake **a**shtrays, you would turn to Chapter A. If **b**owls were your interest, then the relevant chapter would be B, but if it were **v**ases that you wanted to look at, then you would flip to Chapter V. Since the chapter letter designations as well as chapter names are shown as a running head on every other page of Part Two, you generally will be able to locate the chapter you want within seconds.

This is only part of the story, however, because the book is not organized like a dictionary with each piece located in a sequence determined by the first letter of the term used to identify, name or describe it. Rather, the pieces shown in this book have been grouped into a small number of fairly broad *functional* categories, one to each chapter of Part Two. Chapter A, for instance, does not consist entirely of photographs of ashtrays. Included in it are photos of all items with a close functional link to smoking—a fact that is expressed by the full name of Chapter A (Ashtrays and Other Items Related to Smoking). In addition to ashtrays, Chapter A has photos of cigarette boxes, cigarette holders, cigarette jars, humidors, match holders, pipe stands, smoke sets and tobacco jars.

The story is much the same for all the other chapters, although, in a few instances, the functional basis of a chapter's coherence may not be obvious immediately. Therefore, from time to time and at the start of a chapter, comments may be offered about what has been included or excluded in a chapter. In addition, at the beginning of each chapter there is an alphabetic list of all the kinds of items that will be found, as well as the page numbers on which photos of those pieces are located. Experience shows that, within just a few minutes, most users of the book can learn the few particulars of this organizational approach that need to be mastered. If all else fails, there is an index that you can use to pinpoint the location of desired material of all kinds.

Page Organization

When we read words, in English anyway, we normally "move" from left to right. With the photos in Part Two of this book, however, this rule does not hold. Rather, to "read" *sequentially* the photos on the pages of Part Two of this book, one should begin in the upper left corner of a page and then "move" *down*. At the bottom, one goes back to the top (right) of the page where one again reads down. This is because, in general, the photos have been placed within two unmarked vertical columns of equal size that, together, constitute each of the pages of Part Two.

Caption Organization

All full captions have five elements sequenced as follows:

Photo Number
Description
Dimensions
Backstamp
Value

These caption elements are largely self-explanatory. As an aid to the reader, however, certain matters are reviewed briefly here.

PHOTO NUMBER. Each photo or picture "number" is actually a combination of letters and numerals. First is a letter—the same letter used to designate the chapter in which the photo appears. The letter has mnemonic value vis à vis the pieces shown in the chapter. Next are numerals that designate the sequential position of the photo in that chapter. Thus, a number such as "L.23" would designate the 23rd photo in the "L" or "Lamps, Night Lights and Candleholders" chapter. In this book, the photo numbers for each chapter begin with the number after the last one in the same chapter of my previous book on Noritake collectibles. Thus, because there were 22 photos in Chapter L in the first book, the first photo of Chapter L in this book is L.23.

Sometimes there is more than one photo of a piece, usually to show the back side or to show certain details more clearly. The photo number of these pictures has a letter that follows the sequence numerals. Thus, a photo number like "L.36A" indicates a photo that is, in a sense, a variant of photo "L.36." In this instance, as the full caption in Chapter L indicates, L.36A shows a close up of a portion of the night light in L.36. In a few instances, there may be two alternate photos. This happens to be the case for L.36 and, accordingly, the second alternate L.36 photo is L.36B.

DESCRIPTION. Any words immediately following the photo number will indicate what an item is. In most instances, these words will be the same as one or another of the items in the list of subgroup categories given at the start of each chapter. If there are additional comments about the items shown, they are also inserted at this point in the caption.

DIMENSIONS. Data about dimensions are, by their very nature, approximate. For two reasons, it should not be assumed that other pieces like the ones shown in this book will exhibit exactly the same dimensions. First, variations in size can be expected when items are made of porcelain, both because of the character of porcelain and because of the mass-production techniques used to create these particular porcelains. Second, measurement errors are unavoidable even though, in creating this book, every reasonable effort has been made to be as precise as possible about dimensions.

Dimensions are given in decimal form to the nearest eighth inch (0.13"). Normally, the first dimension given is *overall*, or greatest, height (indicated by the letter "h"). This is followed by *overall* (or greatest) width ("w") and, if available or useful, depth ("d"). *Diameter* is given only for basically flat and *truly* round items such as certain plates without handles, powder puff boxes and the like. Height often is not given for basically flat items such as these. For basically flat objects that are *nearly* round, such as cake plates with small handles, the dimensions given are "width" (at the widest point) *and* "depth" or, if one prefers to think of it this way, as the "other width" across the plate at the widest point *without* the handles.

BACKSTAMP. The identity of most of the backstamps on pieces shown in this book is indicated by the word "Backstamp:" followed by a number with 2 digits to the left of the decimal and from 1 to 3 to the right of it. By far the vast majority of the pieces in this book will have one of three kinds of backstamp:

1. An "M-in-Wreath" type (these are all designated by a number beginning with 2; indeed, about 90% of these will be 27.0 or 27.1),

2. A "Komaru" type (usually designated by the number 16.0, 16.1, etc.)

3. A "Cherry Blossom" type (designated by the number 19.0, 19.1, etc.).

The number to the right of the decimal indicates the color of the backstamp. The four most commonly seen colors are: green (.0), red or maroon (.1), blue (.2), magenta (.3), and teal (.4). Thus, a backstamp number such as 27.1 would be read as indicating that the item shown has a red or maroon "M-in-Wreath" backstamp. Other colors found on other backstamps are designated by other numerals to the right of the decimal. A complete list of the color code used in the backstamps is given above in Chapter 3 (see p. 16).

VALUE. The last numbers in the caption indicate the approximate retail value range in current U.S. dollars of the items shown in the photo. For example, numbers such as $120-150 would indicate an approximate retail value range of U.S. $120.00-$150.00. Sometimes, both ends of the range are *not* indicated numerically. Instead, just the lower end of the range is given. For the night light in L.36, for example, the "$1800+" at the end of the caption indicates that one could expect to see a retail price of *at least* $1800.00 on such a piece. This method of indicating value is reserved for rather unusual items which, so far, have been seen rarely if ever in the Noritake collectibles market.

It is impossible for the value designations to be any more than a rough guide to the current retail value of any of the pieces in this book. The condition of the piece (presumed to be mint in this book), individual preferences, changing fashions and many other factors can have a significant impact on the utility of this information. Neither the publisher nor author is responsible for gains or losses that may occur when using or quoting the opinions expressed on these matters in this book.

Chapter A

Ashtrays and Other Items Pertaining to Smoking

In this chapter are photographs of items directly related in one way or another to smoking. The following specific kinds of items are arranged in the order shown:

Most of the items shown in this chapter obviously belong in it and, by the same token, there are few items in other chapters for which a strong case can be made for placing them here as well. The nearest thing to an exception to this "rule" are various "jars" and "dishes" featuring a figural lady in one form or another. The reader will find items similar to certain of the cigarette jars and ashtrays of this chapter in Chapter D where they are designated "dresser dolls," "pin" or "trinket" dishes and "powder jars." One can fairly reliably differentiate these otherwise rather similar items from the cigarette jars in this chapter by looking at the design and decoration of the piece. The key is whether there is a direct reference to smoking, either in the form of distinct rests for cigarettes in ashtrays or in the artwork on an item, such as a painted or molded cigarette. At the same time, however, it should be noted that not all ashtrays have a distinct rest for the cigarette, a fact most easily seen in four-piece bridge ashtray sets, which often have two trays with rests and two without (e.g., A.18, in my first book on Noritake collectibles).

In terms of style, the motifs one finds on smoking items offer tremendous variety and vitality, although not an impressive amount in what one could call truly Art Deco style, except for one tremendously important form: the depiction of women wearing clothing and hair fashions classically associated with the 1920s. This still is one of the most sought-after kinds of Noritake. Of particular note in this chapter are items A.107, A.127 and A.131.

Among the other pieces shown in this chapter with clear Art Deco qualities are several items with an overall geometric motif, both of a regular (e.g., A.129) or free-form (A.135) nature. A geometric design does not, however, warrant the designation "Art Deco" in and of itself. The dramatic ashtray-match holder shown in A.123 nicely il-

lustrates this, I think. If forced to assign it a style name, I would suggest that its strongest affinities are with pre-1920s Gouda wares. A piece with what might be called a quasi-geometric design that seems to fall squarely within the boundary of that multi-splendored "thing" called Art Deco is the smoke set shown in A.152. Why? Because, as I see it anyway, the design is a version of woven art produced by Native Americans of the American Southwest and, as noted in Chapter 2, many Art Deco designs were inspired directly by works from this rich tradition.

A piece with a fine Deco-ish floral motif is the ashtray shown in A.113. The abstract floral as well as the pale and somewhat unusual background colors contribute to the overall Deco feel this piece has. The strong blue vertical stripes on the short sides are incredibly simple and yet they give a great deal of punch to what otherwise would be a rather dainty piece. Another floral piece with a distinct Deco feel is the cigarette jar shown in A.134 and, again, this work is given additional *oomph* by the addition of thin vertical lines. Speaking of thin, the flat cartoon-like figures on two of the ashtrays in this chapter, A.103 and A.104, are of interest to those who love Deco-era items because they echo works usually associated with Clarice Cliff, one of the great artistic icons of this period. For a wonderful overview of her work, see *Clarice Cliff: The Bizarre Affair* by Leonard Griffin and Louis K. and Susan Pear Meisel (see bibliography).

I cannot conclude this introduction to Chapter A without offering brief comments about just a few other items. First, the motif on the smoke set shown in A.151 is a terrific example of an important theme in post-1925 Noritake. Unfortunately, however, it is one that is not all that common, although collectors are seeking them. I refer to the depiction of women engaged in activities that, in the 1920s, were not exactly traditional. In the case of A.151, it is golf. Second, although all the humidors shown are wonderful examples of the creativity and skill of both Noritake designers and artists, the first three are, it seems to me, especially noteworthy. Third, consider the smoke sets shown in A.148 and A.149. How many sets as striking and complete as these have you seen? Very few if your experience as a Noritake collector or dealer is at all typical. One can only wonder why this should be. Fourth and speaking of sets, I have seen one or another of the four ashtrays shown in A.108–111 from time to time, but this is the only complete one I know of—*and* it includes the original boxes. The boxes may partly explain why the set is still intact. Finally, feast your eyes on the cigarette box, match holder, and ashtray set shown in A.125 and A.125A: a truly remarkable specimen. These are *not*, I hasten to add with emphasis, the only comment-worthy and otherwise wonderful items in this chapter. I invite you to savor each and every one.

A.96 Ashtray with figural element. 4.0"h x 6.0"w. Backstamp: 27.0. $550-650.

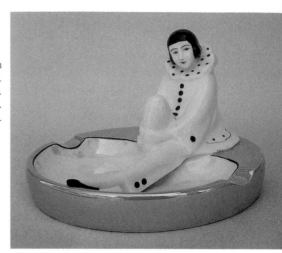

A.97 Ashtray with figural element. 4.0"h x 6.0"w. Backstamp: 27.0. $550-650.

A.97A Detail of A.97.

A.96A Detail of A.96.

A.98 Ashtray with figural element. 3.75"h x 5.13"w x 4.25"d. Backstamp: 27.0. $400-450.

A.98A Detail of A.98.

A.99 Ashtray with figural element. 3.75"h x 6.25"w x 6.0"d. Backstamp: 27.0. $360-400.

A.100 Ashtray with figural element. 2.75"h x 4.88"w. Backstamp: 27.0. $180-250.

A.101 Ashtray with figural element.
2.75"h x 4.75"dia. Backstamp: 27.0.
$180-240.

A.102 Ashtray with
figural element.
3.13"h x 4.5"w. x
2.5"d. Backstamp:
27.1. $80-100.

A.103 Ashtray with figural element. 2.75"h x 5.25"w. x 4.0"d.
Backstamp: 27.1. $240-280.

A.104 Ashtray with figural element. 2.63"h x 5.38"w x 4.0"d.
Backstamp: 27.1. $260-300.

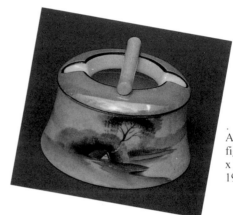

A.105 Ashtray with
figural element. 2.75"h
x 3.88"w. Backstamp:
19.0. $80-100.

A.106 Ashtrays with figural elements. 1.0"h x 5.63"w x 3.13"d.
Backstamp: 27.1. Each, $20-30.

A.107 Ashtray. .63"h x 4.5"w. Backstamp: 27.1. $280-350.

A.110 Ashtray (diamond) with original box. .38"h x 4.75"w x 4.0"d. Backstamp: 29.1. As shown, $180-230.

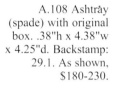

A.108 Ashtray (spade) with original box. .38"h x 4.38"w x 4.25"d. Backstamp: 29.1. As shown, $180-230.

A.111 Ashtray (club) with original box. .38"h x 4.25"w x 4.13"d. Backstamp: 29.1. As shown, $180-230.

A.109 Ashtray (heart) with original box. .38"h x 4.25"w x 3.75"d. Backstamp: 29.1. As shown, $180-230.

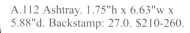

A.112 Ashtray. 1.75"h x 6.63"w x 5.88"d. Backstamp: 27.0. $210-260.

A.112A Detail of A.112.

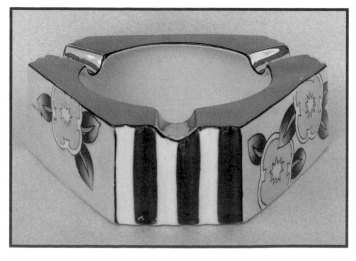

A.113 Ashtray. 1.63"h x 5.0"w. Backstamp: 27.1. $100-150.

A.114 Ashtray. 2.0"h x 3.25"w. Backstamp: 27.0. $60-80.

A.117 Ashtray. 1.5"h x 5.5"dia.
Backstamp: 27.0. $160-190.

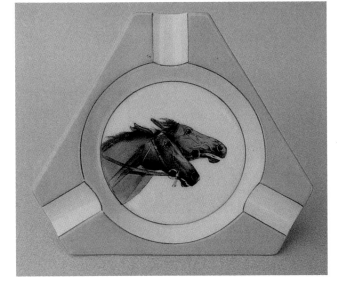

A.115 Ashtray. .75"h x 4.75"dia. Backstamp: 25.1. $90-120.

A.118 Ashtray. 1.25"h
x 5.0"dia. Backstamp:
27.1. $190-240.

A.116 Ashtray. .5"h x 3.5"w x
3.0"d. Backstamp: 27.1. $30-40.

A.116A Side view of A.116.

A.119 Ashtray. 3.0"h x 5.0"w. Backstamp: 27.0. $160-190.

A.122 Ashtray with match holder. 2.0"h x 3.75"w x 2.75"d. Backstamp: 27.1. $180-230.

A.120 Ashtray set. Large tray, 3.5"h x 9.0"w. Ashtrays, .25"h x 3.25"w x 2.75"d. Backstamp (all pieces marked): 27.1. $250-300.

A.123 Ashtray with match holder. 2.0"h x 3.75"w x 2.63"d. Backstamp: 27.1. $90-120.

A.121 Ashtray set in original box. Ashtray 1.13"h x 2.5"w. Box 1.25"h x 7.5"w x 5.0"d. Backstamp: 27.0. As shown, $140-180.

A.124 Ashtray with match holder. 2.0"h x 3.75"w x 2.63"d. Backstamp: 27.1. $90-120.

A.126 Cigarette box/ashtray set. Tray, 1.63"h x 7.5"w x 5.13"d. Box, 1.5"h x 3.5"w x 2.75"d. Ashtrays, .63"h x 3.75"w x 2.38"d. Backstamp: 27.1. $350-450.

A.127 Cigarette box. 1.5"h x 3.63"w x 2.88"d. Backstamp: 27.1. $350-400.

A.125 Cigarette box with match holder. 4.75"h x 4.63"w x 4.5"d. Backstamp: 27.1. $600+

A.125A Alternate view of A.125.

A.128 Cigarette box. 1.63"h x 4.25"w x 3.38"d. Backstamp: 19.1. $120-150.

A.130 Cigarette holder. 3.75"h x 2.5"w x 2.38"d. Backstamp: 27.1. $250-290.

A.129 Cigarette holder. 4.0"h x 2.5"w x 1.88"d. Backstamp: 27.1. $190-230.

A.131 Cigarette holder. 3.88"h x 4.13"w x 2.38"d. Backstamp: 27.1. $250-300.

A.129A Back view of A.129.

A.132 Cigarette holder. 3.0"h x 2.38"w x 2.0"d. Backstamp: 27.1. $190-240.

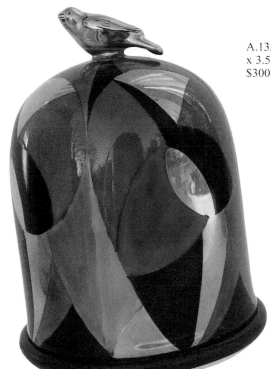

A.135 Cigarette jar. 4.75"h x 3.5"w. Backstamp: 27.1. $300-350.

A.133 Cigarette jar. 5.75"h x 2.75"w. Backstamp: 29.1 (29812). $400-450.

A.136 Cigarette jar. 4.75"h x 3.5"w. Backstamp: 27.0. $180-230.

A.134 Cigarette jar. 5.75"h x 2.75"w. Backstamp: 29.0 (25920). $400-450.

A.136A Back view of A.136.

A.137 Cigarette jars. 5.0"h x 2.75"w. Backstamp: 27.1. Each, $270-320.

A.140 Humidor. 6.0"h x 4.5"w. Backstamp: 27.0. $380-450.

A.138 Humidor. 6.63"h x 4.5"w. Backstamp: 27.0. $400-450.

A.139 Humidor. 6.25"h x 5.0"w. Backstamp: 27.0. $380-450.

A.141 Humidor. 5.75"h x 5.38"w. Backstamp: 27.0. $350-400.

A.139A Back view of A.139.

A.142 Humidor. 5.75"h x 5.38"w. Backstamp: 27.0. $350-400.

A.145 Match holder. 2.75"h x 4.0"w x 2.63"d. Backstamp: 27.0. $70-90.

A.146 Match holder. 2.75"h x 3.75"w x 3.0"d. Backstamp: 07.0. $40-50.

A.143 Humidors. 5.75"h x 5.5"w. Backstamp: *Left*, 27.0; *Right*, 19.1 *Left*, $350-400; *Right*, $300-350.

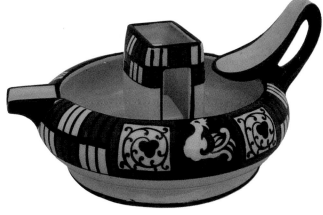

A.147 Pipe stand with ashtray and match holder. 3.25"h x 6.5"w x 5.25"d. Backstamp: 27.0. $180-220.

A.144 Humidor. 4.75"h x 4.0"w. Backstamp: 27.0. $200-250.

A.148 Smoke set. Tray, .5"h x 7.0"dia. Tobacco jar, 3.75"h x 3.5"w. Ashtray, 1.13"h x 3.5"w. Match holder, 2.88"h x 2.25"w x 1.5"d. Backstamp: 27.0. $380-430.

A.149 Smoke set. Tray, .5"h x 6.88"dia. Cigarette jar, 5.0"h x 2.88"w. Match holder, 2.88"h x 2.25"w x 1.5"d. Ashtray, 1.5"h x 2.38"w. Backstamp: 27.0. $300-350.

A.150A Detail of cup in A.150.

A.150 Smoke set. Cigarette cup, 2.25"h x 2.25"w. Tray. .63"h x 7.0"w x 3.5"d. Backstamp: 27.1. $400-450

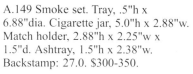

A.151 Smoke set. Cigarette cup, 2.25"h x 2.25"w. Tray. .63"h x 7.0"w x 3.5"d. Backstamp: 27.1. $400-450.

A.151A Detail of cup in A.151.

A.153 Tobacco jar. 3.88"h x 3.25"w. Backstamp: 27.1. $130-200.

A.152 Smoke set. Cigarette cup, 2.25"h x 2.25"w. Tray. .63"h x 7.0"w x 3.5"d. Backstamp: 27.1. $230-290.

Chapter B

Bowls and Boxes

In this chapter, there are photos of over 125 Noritake bowls and boxes. These amazingly diverse materials, which represent only a small fraction of those considered for inclusion in this chapter, have been organized into the categories shown below.

Bowls

Boxes

Organization of the Chapter

As with the other chapters of this book, the primary aim in creating a list like the one above has been to let users of this book locate a specific item as quickly as possible. Given this goal and the large corpus of materials presented in this chapter, it was imperative to use the simplest and most obvious bases for creating categories. Because it is helpful to know what these principles are, I discuss them briefly in the next paragraph, but only as it pertains to the bowls. I do not discuss boxes because they are clustered into only two very simple categories. Since, however, it is not immediately obvious with some items whether one is dealing with a covered bowl or covered box, it should be noted how they are differentiated in this chapter. Covered boxes usually have flat and/or vertical sides; the sides of the bottom half of covered bowls tend to be curved and usually in two directions.

The situation with bowl types, however, is more complex. If you examine the list of bowl types given above, you will see that the bowl types shown have been differentiated with reference to five features. These are (1) whether the bowl has a lid or (2) feet; (3) whether the bowl is round or not; (4) the number and kind of handles (basket or figural); and (5) the purpose of the bowl (general or specific). In the next paragraph, I show how you might use such features to find a particular bowl in this chapter.

Start by thinking about the purpose of the bowl you want to find. If it has or seems to have some obvious and specific purpose (e.g., it is for punch or nuts or celery or salad), then it will be, or at least very probably will be, in a named subgroup of the part of the chapter featuring "Special purpose bowls." If it does not have an obvious specific purpose or function, it will be found within one of the subgroups of general purpose bowls. Most of these bowls are defined in terms of certain very obvious features of a bowl's shape and design. Does it have feet? How many handles does it have? Is it round or does it have sides? With these matters decided, you should be able to use the list given above to pin-point quickly the place in the chapter where the kind of bowl of interest to you is shown.

The Search for Art Deco in Noritake Bowls

The letter B is, obviously, the key to a chapter on "bowls and boxes." This point can be extended to include three words that aptly characterize this collecting area: billions, bargains and boffo. "Billions" because, at times, one feels that there is out there a, virtually, endless supply of Noritake fancy line bowls—seemingly billions and billions of them, to borrow the words of a famous astronomer. "Bargains" because, in general, bowl prices tend to be lower because there are in fact so many of them. "Boffo" because, far more than is usually recognized, some really fine Art Deco designs are found on the humble Noritake bowl. Indeed, I suspect one could do a completely adequate "course" on Art Deco Noritake with just bowls.

In that spirit, turn to photo B.261. It shows three bowls. All three exhibit wonderful examples of the great design work we have come to think of as typical for the Noritake Company during the 1920s. They are, obviously, the same blank and, although some may disagree, I think they are fine examples of three rather different decorative styles. To me, the bowl in the lower right, with its peacock-feather motif and softly curving lines, has a strong Art Nouveau feel. The one on the lower left, however, seems starkly different. The bowl is sharply but unevenly divided; the colors are strong and bluntly contrasting. The flowers are quite unrealistic—they are almost floating near the branch rather than growing from it. These are the sorts of qualities that would lead many collectors to consider this a Deco floral motif, albeit perhaps a notch-or-two down from the upper echelons of such motifs (we will consider some at that high level, shortly). The motif on the remaining bowl in that photo is, in a sense, neither fish nor fowl. Thus, although there is a boldness and elegance to it that should make it appealing to many collectors of Deco florals, the fluidity of the stems may owe something to the Art Nouveau period.

As our search for Art Deco in Noritake bowls continues, let's go back to the beginning—namely, to the first bowl shown in this chapter (B.195). Several key Art Deco stylistic elements practically leap out at us, including the strong, simple colors of the piece as well as its overall boldness of design, coupled with the abstract character of the floral element. One can see how Deco contrasts with the more "modernistic" look that began to dominate in the 1950s, especially in the U.S., by comparing the bowl shown in B.195 with the one shown in B.196. Both seem to involve simple colors and abstract florals. The dominant color of the piece shown in B.196, however (which has a backstamp suggesting that it could well have been made in the 1950s), is not typical of the Deco era. Similarly, the floral element lacks the "edge" and boldness of color and shape that one associates so distinctly with Deco florals.

An extreme example of unusual color and shape for a floral motif is shown in the bowl in B.197. For many, this design will seem downright weird. I happen to like this sort of motif very much (kindred souls in this book include V.224 and Z.38) but many collectors are not comfortable with designs as extreme as this one. A bowl with a somewhat similar design that has strong overtones of the American Southwest is the spectacular punch bowl shown in B.304. There are numerous bowls in this chapter with floral Deco characteristics of a different sort. Of these, I will comment on only two. Both nicely illustrate the way color and form (or composition) contribute to the Deco feel of a piece. First, look at the bowl shown in B.239. The sense of motion, the dramatic difference in the scale of the leaves compared to the stem, but most of all the bold, unrealistic colors and the use of sharp angles (e.g., the saw-toothed edge of the leaves, the yellow triangles on one leaf) combine to make this an eye-stopping design of the first rank. On a par with this bowl is the compote shown in B.287. The design on it appeals to Deco fans for a variety of reasons. For me, part of the intrigue comes from the use of almost pastel shades in a combination of hues that make the piece at once subtle and bold. Some of the other terrific Deco florals in this chapter are shown in B.204, B.207, B.214, B.251, and B.293.

Deco designers often combined various simple, balanced, regular geometric shapes (circles, equilateral triangles, squares) into designs that are just the opposite: complex, unbalanced and irregular. Among the examples in this chapter are the bowls shown in B.254 and B.256. First, it should be noted that all these bowls are superb Deco florals

but for now I should like to focus on the way regular, simple shapes have been combined to create complex and dramatic forms. In B.256, the flowers are bold and vibrant, and yet they are, in essence, a series of overlapping circles. Though more subtle, this is true as well of the two gold fronds in the upper part of the design. In B.254, the most obvious such elements are the bands of gold triangles, again in the upper parts of these designs (see also in this regard, B.224). These designs are similar to another common Deco motif: the zig-zag or lightening bolt. You will look long and hard before you find a better example than the one on the bowl shown in B.241. The use of gold and green in this piece also adds to the Deco feel of it.

Sometimes, geometry will dominate the entire motif, with an effect that, for the lover of Art Deco, is truly exciting, even when the motif itself is quite simple. One of the best examples of this in the entire book is the bowl shown in B.203. The design is "just" some concentric circles, but their varying diameters and widths, plus the colors used, make this a remarkable piece. The effect is only enhanced by the three short legs it sits on (see B.203A), which are, themselves, marvels of geometric simplicity and elegance. In other cases, the geometric motifs found on Noritake-marked porcelains are far more complex. The geometric designs on the lids of the three covered boxes shown in B.314 and B.315 illustrate this nicely. While you are back there, have a look also at the boxes in B.312 and B.313; again, regular shapes are combined to produce vigorous motifs. Sometimes the shape of the bowl itself exhibits these qualities. Two of the better examples in this book are shown in B.206 and B.230. In both, the character of the floral motifs and choice of colors enhance the overall Deco feel of these bowls.

The designs on many Noritake bowls include houses and other structures (e.g., churches, castles, pagodas, bridges). Although I know of no one who has done a precise count, I feel confident in saying that cottages of various kinds are clearly the most common structures found on Noritake-backstamped porcelains from the 1920s. There are undoubtedly several ways to classify types of cottages. The collectors and dealers I know generally distinguish two general types: "Tree-in-the-Meadow" (also known as "T-I-M") type cottages and "Deco cottages." Neither term is ideal but they are in very common use and have more than a little utility, in my opinion. Those unfamiliar with the distinction can best grasp it, I think, by examining and comparing the cottages on the bowls in B.300A and B.316 with those in B.243 and B.260. Interestingly (and this is partly why they have been picked), all these motifs heavily use browns, yellows and other warm colors, but these two sets of bowls differ fundamentally in tone.

One way to refer to the difference is to say that one pair (B.300A and B.316) is quite gentle while the other (B.243 and B.260) is much more forceful. Another contrast is that one is relatively realistic and the other more suggestive. Although all the structures are cottage-like, one pair seems quite rural and the other more urban. Although flowers, trees and other forms of plant life are to be found in all these examples, in one pair they have the feel of food-producing farms, in the other of flower-producing gardens. Perhaps most telling, however, is the way various features on many of the Deco cottage pieces are exaggerated, giving a general boldness and drama to the design. It is at this point, I think, when one comes closest to having grounds for considering these Art Deco motifs. Even so, some may see these as marginal candidates. Indeed, many prefer another common name for such pieces: "cartoon cottages." Whatever the name, there can be no doubt: they have long been and are likely to remain one of the more sought after motif-types to be found on Noritake collectibles and so, if that is your interest,"bowls" is, as they say, "where it's at."

Certain colors and color combinations can contribute greatly to the case for considering a piece Deco. For example, certain greens seem to have been especially favored by the creators of Art Deco designs. Among the examples in this chapter are the bowls and boxes shown in B.241, B.292 and B.313. An important Deco color combination from this period that is shown on a piece in this chapter is green and yellow (see the box in B.317). This item also illustrates an important Deco-era technique for applying colors—namely, the use of an airbrush. This application technique was and still is frequently used to create areas with soft and gradually shifting densities of color. The effects can be striking, indeed, as can be seen in the very unusual compote shown in B.288 and, especially, B.288A. Here, in one superb piece, geometry, color combinations and application technique are combined to produce what is indeed a solid Deco design.

The final Art Deco–related theme to be discussed vis à vis items in this chapter is in many ways the most spectacular. I refer to the several figural items featuring what many collectors refer to, in part for the verbal simplicity of it, as "clowns." Most of these figures depict Pierrot, far and away the most famous member of the legendary *commedia dell'arte*—a comedic improvisational theatrical tradition with roots in Renaissance Italy. To many collectors, items such as the covered bowl in B.295 and the covered boxes in B.308 and B.309 would easily be the most spectacular of the items in this chapter. Unless, that is, they happened to notice the covered box in B.307, which for many is still the Holy Grail of Noritake collecting. But there are so many great ones, how is one to choose?

It would be a serious mistake, however, to conclude from what has been said so far that the non-Deco and non-Pierrot Noritake bowls and boxes lack design strength or desirability. Every item in this chapter has something to recommend it and there are many truly spectacular non-Deco items that I should like to discuss but will not because I simply do not have enough space. I will, though, direct your attention to a few of them simply to give you an idea of some of the other glories that await you in these pages: consider B.225 and B.232, for example or, to pick two contrasting examples, B.235 and B.245. These are truly very fine bowls. But these are just my picks. Now it's your turn to take a look at the many brilliant bowls and boxes on display in this chapter.

Bowls

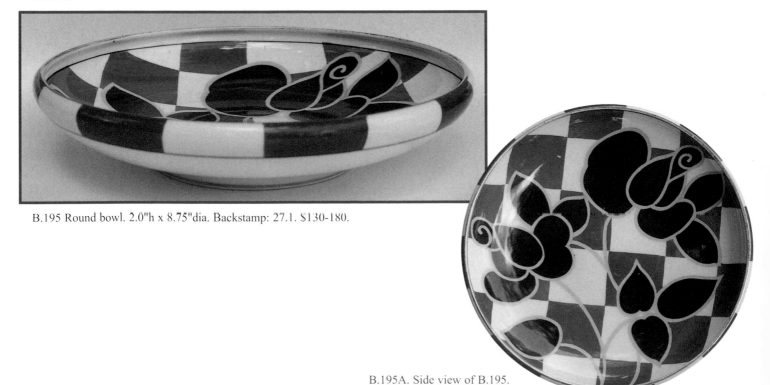

B.195 Round bowl. 2.0"h x 8.75"dia. Backstamp: 27.1. $130-180.

B.195A. Side view of B.195.

B.198 Round bowl. 2.75"h x 8.0"dia. Backstamp: 27.0. $170-220.

B.196 Round bowl. 2.5"h x 11.0"dia. Backstamp: 50.3. $110-140.

B.196A. Side view of B.196.

B.198A. Top view of B.198.

B.199 Round bowl. 1.5"h x 7.13"dia. Backstamp: 29.7 (20056). $30-50.

B.197 Round bowl. 3.0"h x 9.0"dia. Backstamp: 27.0. $150-180.

B.202 Round bowl. 2.88"h x 5.88"w. Backstamp: 19.0 and 27.0. $40-70.

B.200 Round bowl, with three legs. 2.75"h x 6.75"dia. Backstamp: 27.0. $50-70.

B.202A Backstamp(s) on B.202.

B.201 Round bowl, with three legs. 2.75"h x 6.75"dia. Backstamp: 27.0. $50-70.

B.203 Round bowl with 3 legs. 2.0"h x 6.5"dia. Backstamp: 25.1. $100-140.

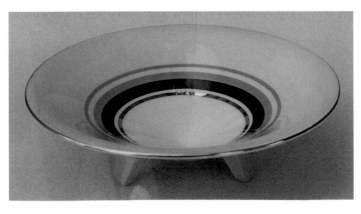

B.203A. Side view of B.203.

B.204 Sided bowl. 2.25"h x 9.5"w. Backstamp: 16.0. $140-170.

B.206 Sided bowl. 2.25"h x 7.0"w x 7.0"d. Backstamp: 27.1. $120-150.

B.205 Sided bowl. 2.5"h x 5.38"w x 5.38"d. Backstamp: 27.0. $110-140.

B.207 Sided bowl, with three ball feet. 2.25"h x 7.38"w x 6.5"d. Backstamp: 27.1. $120-150.

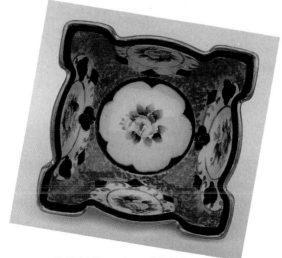

B.205A Top view of B.205.

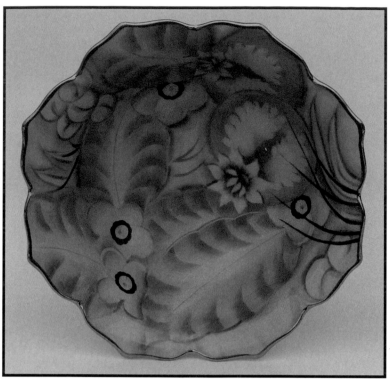

B.208 Sided bowl. 2.5"h x 8.0"w. Backstamp: 27.1. $100-140.

B.210 Basket bowl. 5.0"h x 4.5"w x
4.5"d. Backstamp: 27.1. $170-200.

B.209 Sided bowl. 1.5"h x 8.0"dia.
Backstamp: 25.1. $60-90.

B.211 Basket bowl. 5.75"h x 8.0"w. Backstamp: 27.1. $110-140.

B.212 Basket bowl. 5.75"h x 8.0"w. Backstamp: 19.1. $110-140.

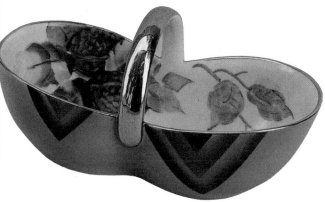

B.215 Basket bowl. 3.5"h x 7.0"w x 3.63"d. Backstamp: 27.1. $130-160.

B.213 Basket bowls. 3.75"h x 3.5"w x 2.5"d. *Center*, Backstamp: 27.0. *Right* and *left*, Backstamp: 27.1. Each, $90-120.

B.214 Basket bowl. 3.0"h x 6.5"w x 4.0"d. Backstamp: 27.0. $100-140.

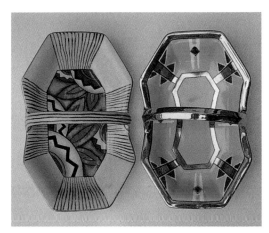

B.216 Basket bowls. 3.38"h x 7.88"w x 4.88"d. Backstamp: 27.1. Each, $100-140.

B.217 Bowls with figural handle. 5.5"h x 7.0"w x 4.5"d. *Left*, Backstamp: 27.1. *Right*, Backstamp: 19.2. Each, $190-240.

B.218 Detail of B.218.

B.217A Detail of B.217, left.

B.218 Bowl with figural handle. 5.0"h x 8.25"w x 3.0"d. Backstamp: 27.1. $120-170.

B.219 Bowl with figural handle. 4.0"h x 6.5"w x 4.5"d. Backstamp: 07.0. $170-190.

B.222 Bowl with figural handle. 2.25"h x 8.75"w x 7.38"d. Backstamp: 27.0. $90-120.

B.220 Bowl with figural handle. 3.63"h x 7.25"w. Backstamp: 27.0. $180-200.

B.223 Bowl with figural handle. 4.0"h x 4.0"w x 3.13"d. Backstamp: 29.1. $90-120.

B.221 Bowl with figural handle. 2.75"h x 6.75"w. Backstamp: 19.1. $120-170.

B.224 Bowl with figural handle. 4.0"h x
8.5"w. Backstamp: 19.0. $100-140.

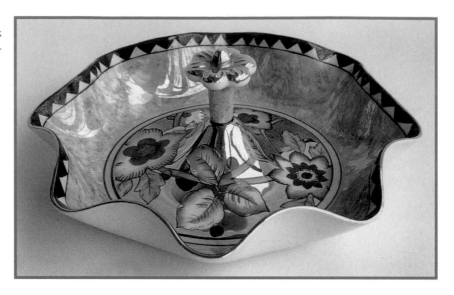

B.227 Bowl with one handle. 3.75"h x 8.0"w x
6.63"d. Backstamp: 19.1. $100-130.

B.225 Bowl with one handle. 2.0"h x 10.5"w x 9.0"d. Backstamp:
27.0. $120-150.

B.226 Bowl with one handle. 2.0"h x 10.5"w
x 9.0"d. Backstamp: 27.0. $120-150.

B.226A Detail of B.226

B.227A Top view of B.227.

B.229 Bowl with one handle. 1.38"h x 6.5"w x 6.25"d. Backstamp: 27.1. $50-80.

B.227B Detail of B.227.

B.230 Bowl with two handles. 2.25"h x 11.5"w x 8.5"d. Backstamp: 16.1. $400+

B.228 Bowl with one handle. 1.88"h x 8.0"w x 7.38"d. Backstamp: 27.1. $50-80.

B.231 Bowl with two handles. 2.0"h x 10.0"w x
8.5"d. Backstamp: 27.0. $160-200.

B.232 Bowl with two handles. 3.38"h x 9.75"w x 9.25"d.
Backstamp: 27.0. $190-240.

B.232B Detail of B.232.

B.232A Top view
of B.232.

B.233 Bowl with two handles. 1.88"h x 9.75"w x 8.88"d.
Backstamp: 27.0. $230-280.

B.235 Bowl with two handles. 2.13"h x 9.25"w x 8.25"d.
Backstamp: 27.1. $150-170.

B.234 Bowl with two handles. 2.13"h x 9.25"w x 8.25"d.
Backstamp: 27.1. $320-350.

B.234A Detail of B.234.

B.236 Bowl with two handles. 3.0"h x 9.75"w x
8.13"d. Backstamp: 27.1. $110-140.

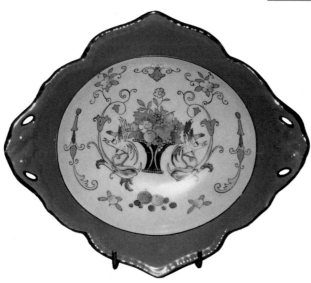

B.237 Bowl with two handles. 1.75"h x 8.25"w x 7.25"d.
Backstamp: 16.2. $60-90.

B.238 Bowl with two handles. 2.0"h x 9.5"w x 8.0"d.
Backstamp: 27.1. $130-180.

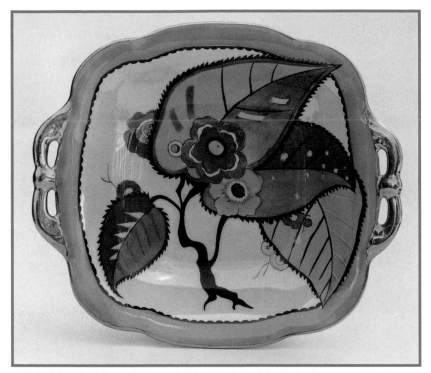

B.239 Bowl with two handles. 2.0"h x 8.0"w x 7.25"d. Backstamp: 27.1. $120-150.

B.242 Bowl with two handles. 2.25"h x 8.25"w x 8.0"d. Backstamp: 27.1. $120-160.

B.240 Bowl with two handles. 1.75"h x 9.75"w x 8.75"d. Backstamp: 27.1. $80-100.

B.241 Bowl with two handles. 2.0"h x 8.0"w x 7.38"d. Backstamp: 16.0. $140-170.

B.243 Bowl with two handles. 1.88"h x 8.0"w x
7.5"d. Backstamp: 27.0. $90-120.

B.244 Bowl with two handles and three ball feet. 1.75"h x 7.5"w x 5.5"d.
Backstamp: 27.0. $190-240.

B.244A Detail of B244.

B.245 Bowl, molded in relief, with two handles. 3.88"h x 10.0"w x 8.0"d. Backstamp: 27.1. $150-190.

B.246 Bowl, molded in relief, with two handles. 3.5"h x 7.75"w x 5.75"d. Backstamp: 27.1. $110-150.

B.247 Bowl with two handles. 2.88"h x 9.5"w x 8.13"d. Backstamp: 25.1. $120-160.

B.248 Bowl with two handles. 1.63"h x 9.25"w x 7.88"d. Backstamp: 27.1. $80-100.

B.249 Bowl with two handles. 1.5"h x 7.38"w x 6.25"d.
Backstamp: 27.0. $70-90.

B.252 Bowl with two handles. 1.5"h x
7.75"w x 6.75"d. Backstamp: 27.1. $60-80.

B.250 Bowl with two handles. 1.5"h x
8.25"w x 6.63"d. Backstamp: 27.3. $80-110.

B.251 Bowl with two handles. 1.5"h
x 7.75"w x 6.75"d. Backstamp: 27.1.
$150-170.

B.253 Bowl with two handles. 2.0"h x 7.38"w x 6.63"d. Backstamp: 27.1. $90-120.

B.253A Detail of B.253.

B.254 Bowls with two handles. 2.0"h x 7.38"w x 6.63"d. Backstamp: 27.1. Each, $120-150.

B.255 Bowl with two handles. 2.25"h x 7.25"w x 6.25"d. Backstamp: 27.0. $40-60.

B.256 Bowl with two handles. 2.0"h x 7.0"w x 6.0"d. Backstamp: 27.0. $100-150.

B.259 Bowl with two handles. 2.63"h x 10.5"w x 9.5"d. Backstamp: 16.2. $250-280.

B.257 Bowl with two handles. 2.0"h x 7.0"w x 6.0"d. Backstamp: 27.0. $80-100.

B.259A Detail of B259.

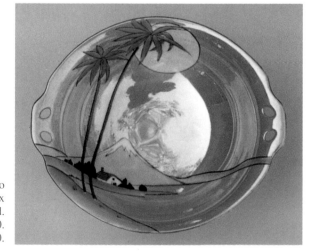

B.258 Bowl with two handles. 2.0"h x 7.0"w x 6.0"d. Backstamp: 27.0. $80-100.

B.260 Bowl with two handles. 2.0"h x 7.5"w
x 6.5"d. Backstamp: 27.1. $100-140.

B.260A Detail of B260.

B.261 Bowls with two handles. 1.75"h x 6.75"w x 6.0"d. Backstamp,
Lower right: 27.0; *Others*, 27.1. Each, $60-90.

B.262 Bowl with two handles.
2.25"h x 7.0"w x 6.13"d. Backstamp:
27.1. $60-90.

B.263 Bowl with two handles. 1.75"h x 6.63"w x 5.38"d. Backstamp: 27.1. $40-60.

B.266 Bowl with two handles. .63"h x 5.75"w x 5.38"d. Backstamp: 25.1. $100-150.

B.264 Bowl with two handles. 1.75"h x 6.63"w x 5.38"d. Backstamp: 27.1. $40-60.

B.267 Bowl with two handles. 2.25"h x 9.0"w x 6.5"d. Backstamp: 27.0. $80-100.

B.268 Bowl with two handles. 2.75"h x 7.5"w x 7.5"d. Backstamp: 25.1. $110-150.

B.268A Side view of B.268.

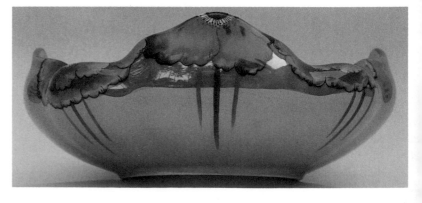

B.265 Bowl with two handles. 1.25"h x 5.5"w x 4.88"d. Backstamp: 16.0. $70-100.

B.269 Bowl with two handles. 2.75"h x 7.5"w x 7.5"d. Backstamp: 27.1. $110-150.

B.271 Bowl with two handles. .75"h x 5.88"w x 5.88"d. Backstamp: 25.1. $40-60.

B.270 Bowl with two handles. 1.5"h x 9.25"w x 8.25"d. Backstamp: 07.0. $90-120.

B.270A Detail of B.270.

B.272 Bowl with three handles. 1.13"h x 5.75"w x 5.5"d. Backstamp: 27.1. $100-140.

B.273 Bowl with three handles. 2.0"h x 9.5"w. Backstamp: 27.1. $90-120.

B.274 Bowl with three handles. 2.0"h x 8.38"w. Backstamp: 27.1. $120-150.

B.273A Detail of B273.

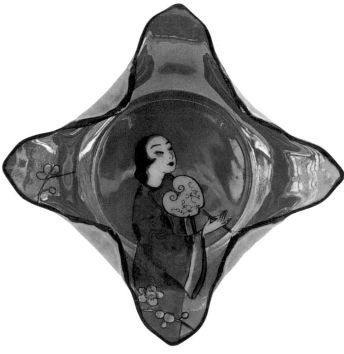

B.275 Bowl with four handles. 1.5"h x 4.75"w. Backstamp: 27.1. $150-190.

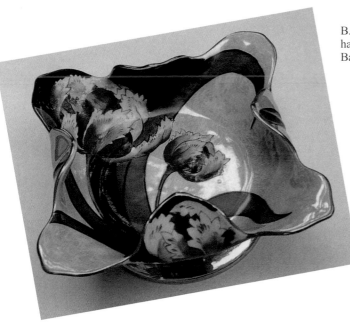

B.276 Bowl with four handles. 3.0"h x 5.5"w. Backstamp: 27.1. $120-140.

B.277 Bowl with four handles. 2.5"h x 9.13"w x 8.38"d. Backstamp: 25.1. $100-140.

B.278 Celery or relish bowl. 1.5"h x 12.5"w x 6.0"d. Backstamp: 27.1. $280-320.

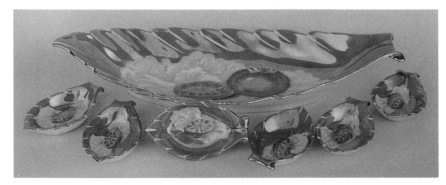

B.279 Celery or relish set. Bowl, 2.75"h x 12.75"w x 5.38"d. Dips, .75"h x 3.5"w x 2.0"d. Backstamp: 27.1. Set, $110-150.

B.279A Detail of B.279.

B.280 Celery or relish bowl. 2.25"h x 12.25"w x 6.13"d. Backstamp: 27.0. $70-100.

B.281 Celery or relish set. Bowl, 1.75"h x 7.13"w x 6.25"d. Dips, 1.0"h x 1.5"w. Backstamp: 27.1. Set shown, $90-120.

B.282 Celery or relish bowl. 2.0"h x 12.0"w x 6.5"d. Backstamp: 19.1. $60-90.

B.283 Compote with handles. 3.38"h x 11.13"w x 9.38"d. Backstamp: 27.0. $130-170.

B.284 Compote with handles. 3.38"h x 11.13"w x 9.38"d. Backstamp: 27.0. $110-140.

B.285 Compote with handles. 3.5"h x 9.5"w x 8.25"d. Backstamp: 16.2. $90-120.

B.286 Compote with handles. 2.75"h x 9.5"w
x 7.75"d. Backstamp: 27.1. $100-140.

B.287 Compote with handles. 2.5"h x 8.5"w
x 7.0"d. Backstamp: 27.1. $190-220.

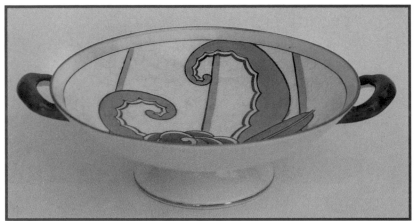

B.287A Detail of B.287.

B.288 Compote with handles. 2.5"h x 8.5"w
x 7.0"d. Backstamp: 27.1. $190-220.

B.288A Underside of B.288.

B.289 Compote with handles. 2.38"h x 6.88"w x 5.75"d. Backstamp: 27.0. $100-120.

B.291 Compote without handles. 6.75"h x 6.88"w. Backstamp: 27.1. $600-700.

B.290 Compote without handles. 6.88"h x 9.13"w. Backstamp: 27.0. $190-220.

B.290A Detail of B.290.

B.292 Compote without handles. 3.5"h x 7.5"w. Backstamp: 27.1. $240-290.

B.294 Compote without handles. 2.88"h x 6.5"w. Backstamp: 27.0. $80-100.

B.293 Compote without handles. 2.88"h x 6.5"w. Backstamp: 27.1. $170-190.

B.295 Covered bowl. 7.0"h x 7.13"w. Backstamp: 27.1. $1500+

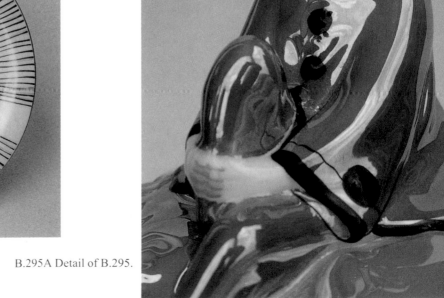

B.293A Top view of B.293.

B.295A Detail of B.295.

B.296 Covered bowl. 5.25"h x 6.63"w. Backstamp: 27.1. $230-280.

B.298 Covered bowl (no notch for a spoon).
5.0"h x 5.0"w. Backstamp: 27.1. $100-150.

B.297 Covered bowl. 4.25"h x 8.0"w x 6.25"d. Backstamp: 27.1.
$110-150.

B.299 Covered bowl.
4.5"h x 5.0"w.
Backstamp: 27.1.
$270-320.

B.299B Detail of B.299.

B.299A Top view
of B.299.

B.300 Cracker bowl. 2.5"h x 8.75"w x
3.5"d. Backstamp: 27.1. $110-140.

B.300A Top view of B.300.

B.301 Jam bowl set. Master bowl,
1.5"h x 7.13"w x 5.5"d. Individual
bowls, 1.0"h x 2.88"w. Backstamp:
27.0. Set, $130-170.

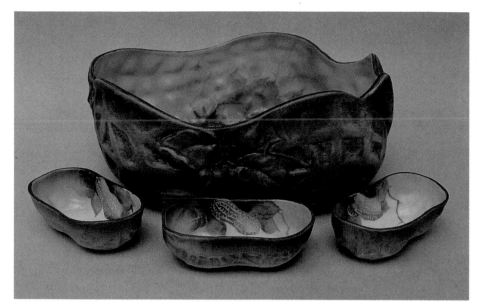

B.302 Nut bowl set (molded in relief). Master bowl, 3.0"h x 7.5"w x 6.63"d. Individual bowls, 1.0"h x 3.0"w x 1.63"d. Backstamp: 27.0. Set, with six individual bowls, $180-200.

B.303 Punch bowl (two pieces). 9.13"h x 16.5"w x 13.5"d. Bowl has no backstamp. Base, Backstamp: 27.1. $1200+

B.303A Back view of B.303.

B.304 Punch bowl (two pieces). 9.13"h x 16.5"w x 13.5"d. Bowl has no backstamp. Base, Backstamp: 27.0. $1200+

B.304A Back view of B.304.

B.305 Salad bowl with serving utensils. Bowl, 4.25"h x 7.75"w. Underplate, 1.5"h x 11.0"dia. Fork and spoon, 1.88"w x 7.25"long. Underplate has no backstamp. Bowl, fork and spoon, Backstamp: 27.1. $180-200.

B.306 Salad bowl with serving utensils. 3.13"h x 7.88"w. Backstamp: 27.1. $160-180.

Boxes

B.307 Covered box. Described as a cigarette box in *Collecting Art Deco Ceramics* (Watson and Watson 1993, p.103), where a similar piece is shown incorporated into a table lamp. 7.0"h x 5.0"w x 4.0"d. Backstamp: 29.1 (29812). $2000+

B.309 Covered box. 5.5"h x 3.63"w. Backstamp: 27.1. $800

B.308 Covered box. 5.5"h x 3.63"w. Backstamp: 27.0. $800

B.308A Detail of B.308.

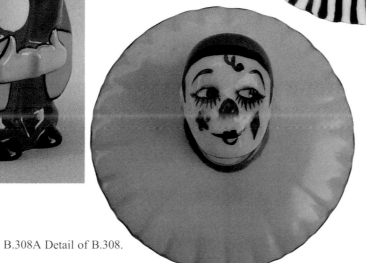

B.309A Detail of B.309.

B.312 Covered box. 4.25"h x 4.5"w x 3.25"d. Backstamp: 27.1. $500-550.

B.310 Covered box. 6.5"h x 5.13"w x 2.25"d. Backstamp: 25.0 (Hotel McAlpin New Year's Eve 1931). $500+

B.310A Bottom of B.310

B.311 Covered box. 2.75"h x 5.38"w x 4.38"d. Backstamp: 65.019. $250-300.

B.313 Covered box. 4.25"h x 4.5"w x 3.25"d. Backstamp: 16.0. $500-550.

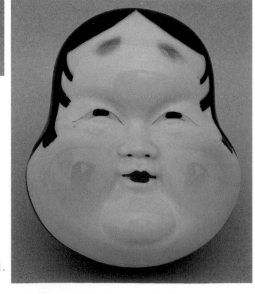

B.311A Top view of B.311.

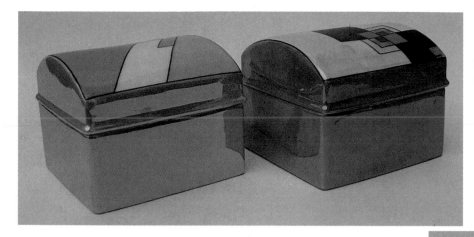

B.314 Covered boxes. 2.75"h x 3.25"w x 3.13"d. Backstamp: 27.1. Each, $200-250.

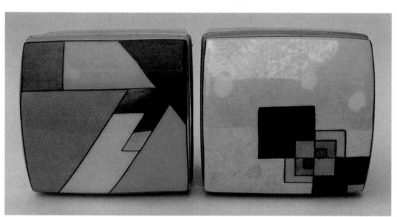

B.314A Top view of B.314.

B.317 Covered box. 4.0"h x 6.5"w. Backstamp: 25.1. $170-200.

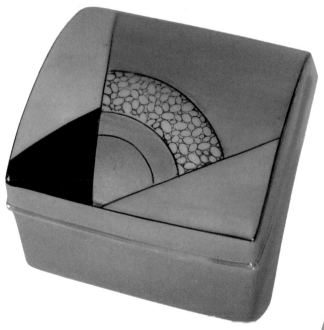

B.315 Covered box. 2.75"h x 3.25"w x 3.13"d. Backstamp: 27.1. $200-250.

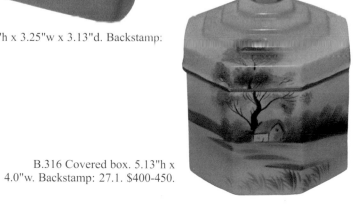

B.316 Covered box. 5.13"h x 4.0"w. Backstamp: 27.1. $400-450.

B.318 Covered box. 2.0"h x 3.75"w. Backstamp: 27.1. $170-200.

Chapter C

Condiment Sets and Related Items

The items shown in the photos of this chapter share this common feature: they all were intended for use in the storing and serving of condiments—i.e., things one normally eats *with* food, *not as* food. Specifically, one will find:

Cream and sugar sets, which admittedly could logically have been included in the above list, are instead shown in Chapter T because of their obvious functional link to the primary focus of that chapter (tea sets and other items pertaining to beverages). A fuller discussion of the reasons for this and other decisions regarding the scope of this chapter was provided in my first Noritake book and will not be rehearsed here. Instead, we may turn our attention to the amazingly intricate and eye-catching world of Noritake "smalls"—a collecting area that apparently is becoming increasingly popular. Space limits are a reality for us all!

Some complete condiment sets are fairly simple. Berry sets, for example, are usually considered complete with just two pieces, the creamer and muffineer (or sugar), though sets with matching trays are known. Most condiment sets, however, are far more complex with numerous small and incredibly fragile lids and spoons. In the course of normal use, or even during storage, these pieces were frequently broken or lost. As a result, complete sets are fairly difficult to come by and accordingly are highly prized. In the face of this, some collectors resort to the long-shot strategy of buying incomplete sets and even single pieces (a tray, spoon or lid for example). The hope is that, in time, these odds and ends can be combined to form a complete set. Almost as improbable is the hope of finding an incomplete set selling at a bargain price that just happens to need one or two pieces you happen to have. Although difficult, this can be done. Indeed, after several years of patience and trades made with collector friends 3,000 miles apart, I myself can say "been there, done that." The results are shown in C.129. I began

with the large duck. For mostly obvious reasons, however, it is no one's preference as a way to collect.

In addition to the low probability of success, another risk in the above "strategy" is that pieces may be combined that do not truly belong together. Sometimes, the impact of this is small—e.g., when the tiny mustard spoon may not have a small stripe of color matching the underplate. In some cases, however, the problem may be greater. For example, perhaps the birds in my "set" originally were on a blue luster tray (the one in C.129 is tan). Because company records or other similar sources that might be able to settle this matter are not available, at present, one is forced into considering other factors. Thus, because the ducks are decorated in both blue and tan luster (and indeed several other colors as well—hence its appeal to me), I concluded that it would have been reasonable for the Noritake Company to use a tray of either color. Indeed, had I found a blue luster tray, I would have used it just as happily. But what about the shape of the tray? Is the one shown in C.129 the right one? The other pieces would fit on most if not all of the other condiment set trays in this and other books. Could I have used one of those and called my "set" a set? There probably are almost as many responses to this as there are collectors and dealers! Personally, I would not accept any other tray because experience tells me that nearly all obviously complete small duck condiment sets are on trays like the one in C.129.

Cynical collectors (a redundancy according to some who obviously are even more cynical; realists according to others) often refer to a pseudo-set as a "marriage"—i.e., an intimate relationship between the unrelated and/or mismatched that do not really belong together. Some "marriages" are fairly easy for the experienced collector to spot. I guess you could say they are really bad marriages. Sometimes, however (and this is one of the things that makes collecting so much fun), it takes sharp and experienced eyes to spot them. In my first book, for example, there are two (I probably should say "at least two") photos of items that may well be marriages: C.60 and T.46. In the case of the sauce "set" in C.60, a very good and obviously sharp-eyed friend of mine, an experienced Noritake collector, pointed out two things. First, the "sauce" bowl seems too small for the spoon. Second, it is basically the same as the sugar bowl in the sugar and creamer set shown in photo T.31 (allowing for some measurement error). The case of the "sugar and creamer" in T.46 is somewhat more complex. The "sugar" may well be a jam set without the underplate and the "creamer" a syrup set, also without the underplate. Both items do indeed match known examples of such sets.

The matter is not completely settled having noted this, however. We know that lids and various other components of Noritake fancy wares were used in several rather different contexts, so it is possible (though not therefore plausible) that some odds and ends may have been put together ("married") at the factory. Or this could have happened at the initial point of sale—e.g., by a shopkeeper where Noritake was sold. In addition, customers, to satisfy a preference, may have asked for lids to be switched, if not on sugar bowls, then possibly on clown boxes such as those shown toward the end of Chapter B. Would factory or store marriages be, somehow, more legitimate?

An interesting variant of the process described above is beautifully illustrated by the extremely important condiment set shown in C.128 and C.128A (again, I note that this is not my set, unfortunately). For years, Noritake collectors and dealers have known of such sets. One is shown in C.22, for example, but the spoon in it is out of view. A similar set with a short, tailless spoon that *is* visible in the photo can be seen in Van Patten's book on Noritake, (Second Series, p. 87, Plate 565). For years, collectors and dealers have "known" that such sets were incomplete if they did not have a little spoon, one that in some cases barely came to the top of the bowl portion of the large chicken. Now, however, with the set shown in C.128 and C.128A, we know that this bit of traditional knowledge may be incorrect. In other words, "sets" with the short simple spoons may technically be marriages. We say "may be incorrect" because we do not have conclusive proof that the Noritake Company only used spoons of the kind shown in C.128A in such sets. Whether they did or not, one thing is sure: the big tail is better.

If I could ask a sample of my Noritake collector friends to predict which chapter of this book would show the single most amazing piece in the book, relatively few would predict Chapter C. Yet, that is exactly where you will find this "top-of-the-heap" piece. It also is shown, spoon in, on the cover of this book. I refer to the jam set in C.133. I know many collectors who would be thrilled beyond words to find such a set or, for that matter, *anything* with the motif that is on it. This is not to say that such a motif should appeal to everyone. I actually know people who do not like the motif—a fact that is actually pleasing to those of us who love it (less competition!). This motif appeals to many because it is a *superb* example of Art Deco design. The backstamp on this set, it should be noted, is the same as that found on the few other pieces known with the motif. From this backstamp, we know that it was meant for export to Great Britain. This backstamp also is on pieces with several of the other really extraordinary Deco motifs found on Noritake wares (e.g., the item shown in B.313)—a fact that has led some to wonder why the best Deco wares were shipped to the U.K.? What does it say about American buyers of the 1920s?

There are many other important pieces in this chapter—too many to mention and comment upon here. I will, however, indulge myself to the extent of offering brief comments about the following eight items, taken more-or-less

in the order they appear in the chapter (this is not a case of "horn-tooting" since none of these items is mine). The exquisite berry set in C.112 is unusual for post-1921 Noritake in being textured in spots—e.g., the green of the trees and the yellow flower. Much of the rest of the surface, and particularly the top of the muffineer or sugar, has a wonderful soft almost fuzzy feel. Until I had the privilege of photographing this set, I had not seen the motif or this decorative technique on Noritake. As often happens, however, I encountered another Noritake item with the exact same motif within weeks of seeing (and touching!) this amazing set (e.g., see V. 243, below; the bowl in B.210 displays the same decoration also but I saw it with the muffineer set shown in this chapter).

Speaking of new decorative motifs, the condiment set in C.119 is distinctive in my experience and quite elegant. The pointed cone on the salt is also somewhat unusual. Even more unusual is the figural bear condiment set (C.122), one you will want to compare to the inkwell shown in Chapter D (D.118). Many such sets must have been made but one seldom sees them for sale, perhaps because of the warm sentiments generally associated with teddy bears. Even so, the pumpkin condiment set in C.126 may be even rarer (it is in my experience, at least). The unusual honey pot in C.131 is similar to one shown in my first Noritake book (see C.40). C.131 is the same blank, obviously, but has a decoration that reverses the one in C.40, which, we now know, probably had an underplate similar to the one shown in C.131 (we really do learn something new every day, especially in collecting).

The three "other" jam sets in this chapter (C.134 to C.136) provide an opportunity to comment again on aspects of Art Deco as a decorative style. Four features of C.134 support a claim that it is a strong Deco item: (1) the yellow and green color combination that was rather common in the Deco-era, (2) the fact that the yellow has obviously been applied by air-brush, (3) the use of silver triangles in the applied decoration and, finally, (4) the angular character of the attached underplate. The case for C.135 is similar: (1) the cream and red color combination, as typical of the era as the yellow and green of C.134, (2) the formal, columnar character of the jar and (3) the inspired simplicity and elegance of the solid semi-circular handle. The third jam set (C.136), which in its own way is as stunning and impressive as the others, simply cannot be considered an Art Deco work. True, it is green, but many would say it is the "wrong" shade. It is the lid, however, that is the key point. If the fruit were painted in unnatural, "impossible" colors, one *might* be tempted, but with their realistic shapes, even that might not be enough.

Although I have the strongest urge to say a few words about every one of the figural salt and pepper sets, I will do no more than encourage you to do what you almost certainly will do anyway, which is admire them greatly, for they really are wonderful items. I must comment about one salt and pepper set, though—namely, the set shown in C.160 and C.160A—an item that, amazingly enough (given all that was said above about sets and marriages) is not a true set! Even so, I believe it is one of the more important items shown in this book. This is because it is the only instance known (so far, let us hope) of a piece with a Noritake M-in-Wreath backstamp *embossed in metal!* It is a marriage rather than a true set because the salt and pepper have non-Noritake backstamps ("Japan" in black) —a fact I overlooked in the excitement of taking these photographs.

But don't focus exclusively on the items mentioned above. Each piece shown in this chapter, even the smallest (indeed, for many, especially the smallest), is a "mighty-mite" in its own right with much to recommend it.

C.112 Berry set. Sugar, 7.0"h x 3.0"w. Creamer, 6.25"h x 3.5"w. Backstamp: 25.1. Set, $190-220.

C.110 Berry set. Sugar, 7.0"h x 3.25"w. Creamer, 5.75"h x 4.38"w. Backstamp: 27.1. Set, $150-190.

C.113 Berry set. Sugar, 7.0"h x 3.0"w. Creamer, 6.25"h x 3.5"w. Backstamp: 19.1. Set, $160-200.

C.111 Berry set. Sugar, 6.75"h x 3.0"w. Creamer, 5.75"h x 4.0"w. Backstamp, creamer: 27.1. Backstamp, sugar: MIJ.1 Set, $150-190.

C.114 Berry set. Sugar, 6.5"h x 2.63"w. Creamer, 5.63"h x 3.38"w. Backstamp: 27.1. Set, $170-220.

C.116 Berry set. Sugar, 6.5"h x 2.63"w. Creamer, 5.63"h x 3.38"w. Backstamp: 27.1. Set, $120-180.

C.115 Berry set. Sugar, 6.5"h x 2.63"w. Creamer, 5.63"h x 3.38"w. Sugar, Backstamp MIJ.1. Creamer, Backstamp: 27.1. Set, $260-320.

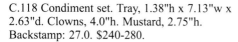

C.117 Butter dish. 3.0"h x 7.63"w. Backstamp: 27.0. $90-120.

C.118 Condiment set. Tray, 1.38"h x 7.13"w x 2.63"d. Clowns, 4.0"h. Mustard, 2.75"h. Backstamp: 27.0. $240-280.

C.119 Condiment set. Tray, 1.38"h x 7.13"w x 2.63"d. Mustard, 2.78"h x 2.0"w. Salt (left), 2.5"h x 1.38"w. Pepper, 2.38"h x 1.25"w. Backstamp: 27.1. $160-180.

C.120 Condiment set. Tray, 1.38"h x 7.13"w x 2.63"d. Mustard, 2.78"h x 2.0"w. Figural salt and pepper, 3.63"h x 1.63"w. Backstamp: 27.0. $120-170.

C.121 Condiment set. 3.0"h x 5.5"w x 4.75"d. Backstamp: 27.0. $220-260.

C.122 Condiment set. The tray has no backstamp. The head of the large bear (mustard or sugar) is removable. Compare this piece to the inkwell shown, below, in D.118. Overall, 3.5"h x 4.38"w. Backstamp: 27.1. $300-350.

C.123 Condiment set. The tray has no backstamp. 3.5"h x 4.38"w x 4.75"d. Backstamp: 27.0. $80-110.

C.126 Condiment set. Tray, 1.25"h x 5.25"w. Mustard, 2.75"h x 2.5"w. Salt and pepper, 1.88"h x 1.88"w. Backstamp: 27.0. $140-190.

C.124 Condiment set. The tray has no backstamp. 3.5"h x 4.38"w x 4.75"d. Backstamp: 27.1. $90-120.

C.127 Condiment set. Tray (no backstamp), .5"h x 6.88"w x 2.88"d. Large bird (no notch for spoon), 3.25"h x 2.25"w. Salt and pepper, 2.38"h 1.63"w. Backstamp: 27.1. $200-250.

C.125 Condiment set. Tray, 1.25"h x 4.75"dia. Mustard, 2.63"h x 2.13"w. Salt and pepper, 2.5"h x 1.5"w. Backstamp: 27.1. $130-180.

C.128 Condiment set. Tray (no backstamp), .5"h x 6.88"w x 2.88"d. Large bird (mustard) 3.75"h x 3.0"w. Salt and pepper, 2.63"h x 1.75"w. Backstamp: 27.0. $300+

C.130 Gravy boat. "Boat," 3.75"h x 6.5"w x 3.13"d. Underplate, .88"h x 6.25"w x 4.5"d. Backstamp (both pieces): 27.0. $50-90.

C.128A Alternate view of C.128 showing the correct and *very rare* mustard spoon which, when placed in the large bird, forms its tail.

C.131 Honey pot. 5.13"h x 3.75"w. Underplate (no backstamp), .63"h x 5.38"dia. Backstamp: 27.1. $200-250.

C.129 Condiment set. Large duck, 1.88"h x 3.0"w x 1.5"d. Small duck, 1.25"h x 1.88"w x 1.13"d. Tray, .75"h x 4.88"w x 3.38"d. Backstamp (tray and large duck), 27.0. $120-180.

C.132 Honey pot. 3.88"h x 2.75"w x 2.5"d. Backstamp: 27.1. $190-230.

C.134 Jam jar with attached underplate. 5.0"h x 5.0"w. Backstamp: 27.1. $160-200.

C.133 Jam set. 6.25"h x 5.5"w. Backstamp: 16.0. $400+

C.135 Jam set. 4.5"h x 5.25"w. Backstamp: 27.1. $130-190.

C.136 Jam set. 4.88"h x 5.63"w. Backstamp: 27.1. $130-190.

C.139 Sauce set. Bowl, 2.25"h x 3.25"w. Underplate, .88"h x 6.5"dia. Backstamp: 25.1. $150-180.

C.137 Sauce set. Bowl, 3.88"h x 5.63"w. Underplate (no backstamp but has molded star with six points) 1.38"h x 10.75"dia. Backstamp: 27.1. $170-210.

C.140 Mayonnaise set. 3.5"h x 6.25"w. Backstamp: 29.1. $80-100.

C.138 Whipped cream set. Bowl, 2.88"h x 5.88"w x 4.88"d. Underplate, 1.0"h x 6.5"dia. Backstamp: 27.1. $120-160.

C.141 Mayonnaise set. 3.25"h x
5.5"w. Backstamp: 27.0. $60-90.

C.144 Mustard pots with attached underplates. 3.5"h x 4.0"w. *Left*,
Backstamp: 27.1. *Right*, Backstamp: 27.0. $80-100.

C.142 Mayonnaise set. 3.13"h x 5.38"w.
Backstamp: 27.1. $90-110.

C.145 Oil and vinegar set. Oil and vinegar bottles, 6.0"h x 3.0"w. Tray,
8.0"w x 4.5"d. Backstamp: 27.1. $120-160.

C.143 Mayonnaise set. 2.63"h x 6.25"w. Backstamp: 27.1. $90-110.

C.146 Salt and pepper sets. 4.5"h x 1.38"w. Backstamp: J.1. Each, $20-40.

C.147 Salt and pepper set. 3.75"h x 1.75"w. Backstamp: MIJ.0. Each, $140-180.

C.149 Salt and pepper set. 1.88"h x 1.63"w. Backstamp: J.1. Each, $80-100.

C.148 Salt and pepper set. 2.5"h x 1.25"w. Backstamp: MIJ.1. Each, $20-40.

C.150 Salt and pepper sets. 4.13"h x 1.25"w. *Left*, Backstamp: J.1. *Right*, Backstamp: J.0. Each, $50-70.

C.151 Salt and pepper sets. 4.13"h x 1.25"w. Backstamp: J.1. Each, $50-70.

C.153 Salt and pepper set. 2.25"h x 1.5"w. Backstamp: MIJ.1. Each, $80-100.

C.152 Salt and pepper set. 3.5"h x 2.0"w. Backstamp: J.0. Each, $80-100.

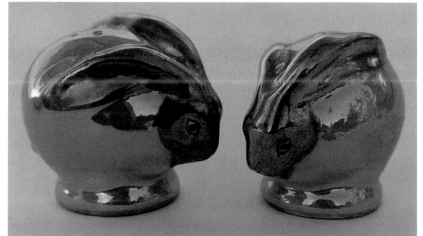

C.154 Salt and pepper set. 1.63"h x 1.75"w. Backstamp: J.0. Each, $70-90.

C.155 Salt and pepper set. 2.88"h x 1.75"w.
Backstamp: J.0. Each, $60-90.

C.158 Salt and pepper set. Tray (has full backstamp), 3.5"h x 4.0"w
x 1.63"d. Salt and pepper, 2.63"h x 1.5"w. Backstamp: 27.0. Set,
$180-230.

C.156 Salt and pepper set. Tray (has no backstamp), 1.13"h x 4.25"w x
2.75"d. Salt and pepper, 2.0"h x 1.63w. Backstamp: J.1. $180-220.

C.157 Salt and pepper set. Tray
(has no backstamp), 1.13"h x
4.25"w x 2.75"d. Pepper shaker,
2.0"h x 1.75"w. Salt dip, 1.13"h x
1.75"w. Backstamp: J.1. Set,
$150-190.

C.159 Salt and pepper set. Tray (has full backstamp), 3.5"h x 4.0"w x 1.63"d. Salt and pepper, 2.75"h x 1.5"w. Backstamp: 27.1. Set, $80-90.

C.160 Salt and pepper set. Metal tray, 2.63"h x 3.25"w x 1.5"d. Salt and pepper, 2.13"h x 1.25"w. Backstamps: tray (embossed in metal), 26.8. salt and pepper, J.5 (Not a Noritake backstamp). Set, $150+

C.162 Salt and pepper set. Tray, 4.38"w x 2.63"d. Pepper, 2.5"h x 1.0"w. Backstamp: 27.0. $50-70.

C.160A Bottom of tray in C.160, showing the only example so far known of a Noritake backstamp embossed in metal.

C.163 Salt and pepper set. Tray, 4.38"w x 2.63"d. Salts and peppers, 1.0"h. Backstamp: 27.1. $280-330.

C.161A View of C.161 showing the open salt.

C.161 Salt and pepper set. 2.63"h x 1.88"w. Backstamp: 27.0. $40-60.

C.164 Salt set in original box. Box, 1.38"h x 5.88"w x 4.25"d. Salts, 1.25"h x 2.13"w x 1.75"d. Backstamp: 27.1. Set, as shown, $200-250.

C.166 Salt set in original box. Box, 1.0"h x 6.13"w x 4.25"d. Salts, .75"h x 2.5"w x 1.88"d. Backstamp: 27.0. Set, as shown, $150-180.

C.165 Salt set in original box. Box label says: 100/ 223 1 1 set Made in Japan. Box, 2.13"h x 5.75"w x 4.88"d. Salts, 1.75"h x 2.0"w x 1.38"d. Backstamp: 27.1. Set, as shown, $200-250.

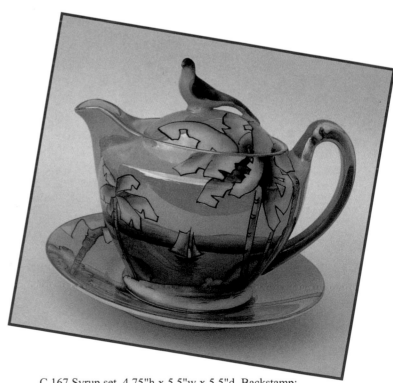

C.167 Syrup set. 4.75"h x 5.5"w x 5.5"d. Backstamp: 27.0. $150-170.

Chapter D

Desk and Dresser Items

In this chapter, one will find photos of the following kinds of items meant for use in the home on and around desks and dressers:

Desk Items

    Ink wells (pp.94-95)

Dresser Items

    Dresser dolls (pp.95-96)
    Dresser sets (pp.96-97)
    Dresser trays (pp.97-100)
    Perfume bottles (pp.100-101)
    Pin trays (p.100)
    Powder boxes and jars (pp.102-103)
    Powder puff boxes (pp.104-106)
    Rouge (or cosmetic) boxes (p.106)
    Talcum powder shaker (p.107)
    Trinket dishes (p.107)

In keeping with the goal of having a small number of alphabetically labeled chapters with items clustered so as to make the chapter letters an easy to use mnemonic device, this chapter has both desk and dresser items in it. There is more to the combination than alphabetical coincidence, however. Both the motifs on and functions of the items in this chapter show that they all were to be used primarily, if not exclusively, by women—a claim that cannot long be sustained for any of the other chapters. In this book, as in the previous one, the emphasis in Chapter D is decidedly on dresser items.

This fact does not constitute a "bias" on my part but, rather, is entirely the result of presumably consumer-driven trends in the Noritake-marked fancy line products of the period covered by this book. To put it starkly: relatively few Noritake-marked desk items are known. Of those shown in this book, the reader should note particularly the ink well in D.119. The basic shape of this piece will be familiar to collectors and dealers with all but the most modest experience in the field. This particular ink well, however, is the only one known, as of this writing, with an attached pen-holder. Speaking of "only knowns," the five owl ink wells in this chapter exhibit the full range of motifs known (at least up to now) on these highly prized items. One always hopes, of course, that new ones will turn up eventually.

With the dresser items, on the other hand, new motifs and forms seem to turn up more often, though far less frequently than collectors and dealers would like, for let's face it: dresser items are one of the hottest single Noritake collecting categories (the only other real contender would be

"lady items"—a motif category that cuts across the functional groupings used to organize this book and which heavily overlaps dresser items). This is reflected in the values for these items, which are relatively high and seem to be rising at a faster than average rate. I have not done the math, but I suspect that the average value of the items shown in this chapter is far higher than for any other chapter.

There are *many* really spectacular items in this chapter—so many I practically get a headache thinking about all the wonderful items I will *not* be saying anything about. Once again, I feel I should emphasize here that, except for powder puff boxes, I have relatively few dresser items in my collection. In other words, I am not simply touting what I happen to be interested in as a Noritake collector. This said, I offer a few brief comments about ten of the more unusual and rare items shown in this chapter. In contrast to several of the other chapters of this book, I do not comment here on those pieces that illustrate various important aspects of Art Deco as a style. I honestly believe the examples are too obvious to warrant it and, were I to start, I would end up saying something about every item in the chapter.

I begin with the dresser doll in D.121. It is very unusual in being so thin front to back—at 1.63 inches, it is less than half its width. This is the only dresser doll in this shape that I have seen, although there must be others. I certainly hope so anyway.

The next dresser doll (D.122) is also unique, so far. The removable top half of this two-piece item is the portion from the green skirt hem up. It is thought to have been used for storing unsightly dresser items, such as hairpins or small, plain perfume bottles.

Ruefully skipping over all the dresser sets and dresser trays, each a Noritake masterpiece in its own right, I turn next to the perfume bottle shown in D.131 and D.131A. I single out this one because, in the first book, a similar looking bottle was shown (D.37 and D.37A). The one in D.131, however, is much smaller (3.75"h. vs. 5.25"h.). As with the other perfume bottle, I marvel that the top halves of any of these pieces have survived at all. Next, take a look at the powder box in D.136 (one of three known to collectors). She is obviously the "sister" of the powder box (D.58) that graced the cover of my first Noritake book.

Powder puff boxes are, I admit, one of my special interests and so I will not deny it: this chapter has 14 superb examples partly because of this. The first two (D.142 and D.143), like the powder boxes just mentioned, are obviously "sisters," not only vis à vis each other but also to one shown in my first Noritake book (see D.79). The really remarkable thing about D.142, however, is that it was found with the original box—a spectacular first for such a piece so far as I know. I cannot resist mentioning the third puff box shown (D.144). Seeing one just like it nearly 20 years ago (in mid-1979) is what set me off in search of my own Noritake. Friends of mine had recently purchased their piece for an amount they "knew" to be excessive at the time—$10! I am still looking for mine. Next, note the puff boxes in D.152—interesting mirror images of a woman gazing in a mirror. Finally, I must direct your attention to the faces on the last two items in this chapter (D.160 and D.161). The first of these pin trays (they are not considered ashtrays because there are no rests for cigarettes) is well known to many collectors, not because it is common (far from it!) but because it is so striking and, well, memorable. Interestingly, though, because of the angle of the head, one must make quite an effort even to see the face on it in those *few* situations where it is on view. With photo D.160A, the task is made easier. Finally, consider D.161A: is that a face or what?

Well, now you know what got my attention in this chapter. It is time for you to discover which of these great pieces do it for you.

D.116 Ink well. 3.5"h x 2.63"w. Backstamp: 27.0. $240-280.

Desk Items

D.117 Ink wells. 3.5"h x 2.63"w. *Left,* Backstamp: 27.1; *Others,* Backstamp: 27.1. *Left* and *center*, each, $250-280; *Right*, $230-250.

D.115 Ink well. 3.5"h x 2.63"w. Backstamp: 27.1. $500.

Dresser Items

D.118 Ink well. 3.88"h x 3.13"w. Backstamp: 27.1. $400+

D.120 Dresser doll. 6.25"h x 3.63"w. Backstamp: 29.1 (29812). $650-750.

D.118A View of D.118 showing interior.

D.119 Ink well. 4.5"h x 3.75"w. Backstamp: 27.1. $400+

D.121 Dresser doll. 4.75"h x 4.0"w x 1.63"d. Backstamp: 19.1. $300-350.

D.124 Dresser set. Tray, .63"h x 10.25"w x 7.0"d. Powder jar, 4.75"h x 4.0"w. Powder puff box, .88"h x 3.25"dia. Powder jar, Backstamp: 29.1 (25920). Others, Backstamp: 27.1. Set, as shown, $600-700.

D.122 Dresser doll. .5.0"h x 2.0"w. Backstamp: 27.1. $280-340.

D.123 Dresser set. Tray, .63"h x 10.75"w x 7.38"d. Powder jar, 6.25"h x 4.5"w. Hair receiver, 2.25"h x 3.0"w. Hair pin tray, 1.0"h x 4.13"w x 2.25"d. Backstamp (all items marked): 27.0. Set, as shown, $500-600.

D.125 Dresser set. Tray, .63"h x 10.25"w x 7.0"d. Powder jar, 5.5"h x 4.13"w. Powder puff box, 1.0"h x 4.0"dia. Powder jar, Backstamp: 29.0 (25920). Others, Backstamp: 27.0. Set, as shown, $600-700.

D.126 Dresser tray. .63"h x 10.25"w x 7.0"d. Backstamp: 27.0. $380-440.

D.126A Detail of D.126.

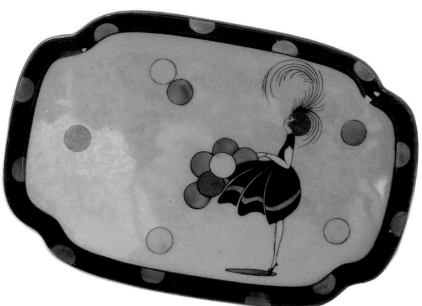

D.127 Dresser tray. .63"h x 10.38"w x
7.13"d. Backstamp: 27.1. $380-440.

D.127A Detail of D.127.

D.128 Dresser tray. 1.0"h x 10.75"w x
6.5"d. Backstamp: 27.1. $450+

D.128A Detail of D.128.

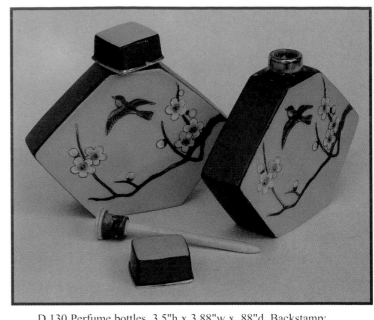

D.129 Dresser tray. .38"h x 8.5"w x 5.75"d. Backstamp: 27.1. $600+

D.130 Perfume bottles. 3.5"h x 3.88"w x .88"d. Backstamp: 27.1. Each, $130-180.

D.131 Perfume bottle. 3.75"h x 1.5"w x 7.13"d. Stopper, 2.5"long. Backstamp: 27.1. $300-350.

D.129A Detail of D.129.

D.131A View of D.131, disassembled.

D.132 Perfume bottles. 5.25"h x 1.88"w. Backstamp: 27.1. Each, $200-250.

D.135 Pin dish. 12.0"h x 3.0"w x 6.5"d. Backstamp: 27.0. $90-130.

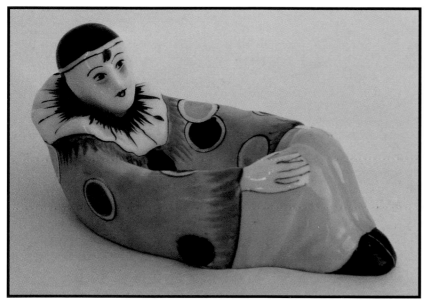

D.133 Pin tray. 2.13"h x 4.5"w x 2.63"d. Backstamp: 27.1. $450-480.

D.134 Pin dish, souvenir of "Menominee Mich."[igan]. 2.0"h x 2.63"w. Backstamp: 27.1. $40-60.

D.136 Powder box. 4.75"h x 4.5"w. Backstamp:
27.1. $750+

D.138 Powder box. 5.5"h x 4.0"w. Backstamp: 29.0
(25920). $410-480.

D.137 Powder box. 5.5"h x 3.38"w.
Backstamp: 29.1 (25920). $430-500.

D.137A Detail of D.137.

D.139 Powder boxs. Left, 5.5"h x 3.38"w. Backstamp: 29.1 (25920). Right, 5.5"h x 4.0"w. Backstamp: 29.0 (25920). Each, $410-480.

D.140 Powder box. 4.25"h x 7.25"w. Backstamp: 25.1. $150-190.

D.141 Powder box 3.0"h x 6.0"w x 4.5"d. Backstamp: 43.056. $130-180.

D.140A Top view of D.140.

D.141A Top view of D.141.

D.142 Powder puff box, with original box. Box, 1.5"h x 4.25"dia w. Puff box, 1.0"h x 4.0"dia. Backstamp: 27.1. $450-550.

D.143 Powder puff box. 1.0"h x 4.0"dia. Backstamp: 27.1. $420-460.

D.145 Powder puff box. 1.0"h x 4.0"dia. Backstamp: 27.0. $420-460.

D.144 Powder puff box. 1.0"h x 4.0"dia. Backstamp: 27.1. $420-460.

D.146 Powder puff box. 1.0"h x 4.0"dia. Backstamp: 27.0. $360-390.

D.147 Powder puff box. 1.0"h x 4.0"dia. Backstamp: 27.1. $330-370.

D.150 Powder puff box. 1.0"h x 3.75"dia. Backstamp: 27.1. $380-430.

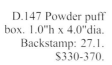

D.148 Powder puff box. 1.0"h x 4.0"dia. Backstamp: 27.0. $190-250.

D.151 Powder puff box. 1.0"h x 3.75"dia. Backstamp: 27.0. $320-360.

D.149 Powder puff box. 1.0"h x 4.0"dia. Backstamp: 27.1. $400-450.

D.152 Powder puff boxes. Both, 1.0"h x 4.0"dia. *Left*, Backstamp: 27.0. *Right*, Backstamp: 27.1. $290-340.

D.155 Rouge jar. 3.0"h x 2.13"w. Backstamp: 27.1. $190-240.

D.153 Powder puff box. .75"h x 4.0"dia. Backstamp: 19.0. $200-250.

D.155A Back view of D.155.

D.154 Powder puff box. 1.25"h x 3.75"dia. Backstamp: 27.1. $120-170.

D.156 Rouge jar. 3.75"h x 3.25"w. Backstamp: 19.2. $130-170.

D.154A Top view of D.154.

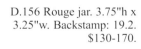

D.160 Trinket dish. 3.5"h x 5.0"w.
Backstamp: 27.1. $800+

D.160A Detail of D.160.

D.157 Talcum powder shaker. 6.25"h x
2.88"w. Backstamp: 27.0. $100-150.

D.161 Trinket dish. 3.5"h x
5.0"w. Backstamp: 27.1.
$440-490.

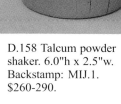

D.158 Talcum powder
shaker. 6.0"h x 2.5"w.
Backstamp: MIJ.1.
$260-290.

D.159 Trinket dish. 4.0"h x 5.13"w.
Backstamp: 19.2. $350-370.

D.161A Detail of D.161.

Chapter F
Figurines

In this chapter are a dozen remarkable Noritake backstamped figurines, sequenced as shown below in the alphabetical list of subgroups consisting of these figurines' basic forms:

The backstamps on many of these pieces tell us (see Chapter 3 for details) that they were made, originally, for the domestic (i.e., the Japanese) market. That they were all found in North America on the collectibles market indicates they have traveled far, in many cases in the bags of Americans returning from military service in Japan. These figurines still represent only a tiny portion of the collections of a small but steadily growing number of Noritake collectors. It is appropriate, therefore, that this is a small chapter. In the future, though, this may change—a prediction we make based on information that is becoming available through Noritake Company sales brochures from the present and very recent past. These materials show scores of similar and often spectacular figural items currently or very recently for sale—again, primarily in Japan. In contrast to the items shown in this chapter, these newer items are, by almost any standard, fairly expensive. They are also hardly what one would call Noritake collectibles in the usual sense of the term. That they will be collectibles one day is certain. When that day comes, the items shown in this chapter will be the "really old" items that started it all.

Several pieces in this chapter deserve comment (well, they *all* deserve it), but I will limit my remarks to five items, taken pretty much in the order they appear in the chapter. First, consider the fish and sea life figurines (F.23 and F.24). Both exhibit a feature that make these porcelain items particularly attractive to many—namely, the use of delicate wisps of porcelain water plants to suspend the fish and seahorses, so they look like they are swimming right before your eyes. The figurine shown in F.25 could have been placed in Chapter L since, in the base at the back of the piece, there is a factory-drilled hole for a lamp cord, thus showing that this superb Deco piece was intended as a lamp base. It was placed in this chapter, however, because most people, on seeing it, think of it as a figurine. Finally, have a look (if you haven't already) at the amazing *vehicle* shown in F. 33 and F.33A. As indicated by what is shown in the photo of the base of this piece (F.33B), the Noritake Company made it (and presumably many others like it) for the Toyota Company. Why? Go figur(ine)!

F.22 Figurine. 10.88"h x 11.63"w. Backstamp: 65.019. $400+

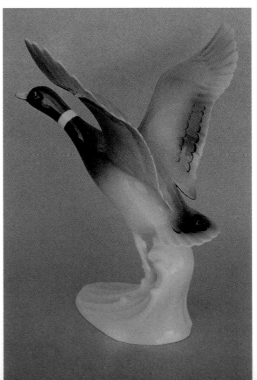

F.22A Reverse view of F22.

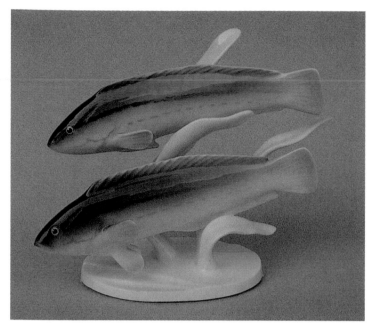

F.23 Figurine. 6.25"h x 7.75"w x 3.0"d. Backstamp: 65.019. $150-170.

F.24 Figurine. 5.88"h x 2.75"w. Backstamp: 65.019. $150-170.

F.25 Figurine. This item has a factory-drilled hole at the base (back) to accommodate a lamp cord. 11.0"h x 4.75"w. Backstamp: 27.1. $700+

F.28 Figurine. 7.75"h x 4.13"w. Backstamp: 65.019. $150-170.

F.26 Figurine. 7.0"h x 5.0"w. Backstamp: 43.056. $190-230.

F.27 Figurines, arranged to show front and back views. 4.25"h x 8.75"w x 4.25"d. Backstamp: 67.019. Each, $250+

F.29 Polar bear figurine. Introduced in
1958. 5.25"h x 8.0"w x 4.5"d. Backstamp:
65.5. $170-190.

F.31 Figurine. 4.25"h x 4.25"w x 3.63. Backstamp: 70.7 (Third
edition, 1 of 2800 Mother's Day 1976). $170-190.

F.30 Figurine. 5.63"h x 7.5"w x 2.38"d.
Backstamp: 65.019. $150-180.

F.32 Figurine. 4.38"h x 3.13"w. Backstamp:
78.9. $150-180.

F.33 Figurine. 4.25"h x 8.75"w x 4.25"d.
Backstamp: 65.5. $500+

F.33A Opposite side
view of F.33.

TOYOTA MOTOR CO., LTD.

F.33B Bottom view of F.33.

Holiday and Special Occasion Items

Unlike the other chapters of this book, I do not list the items in it at the start, mostly because this chapter is so small. There are only nine items in it and, except for the first one (more about this in a moment), all are Father's and Mother's Day pieces produced in the 1970s by the Noritake Company as a collector series.

Since "special occasions" is one of the unifying themes of this chapter, virtually all of the items in this book could be candidates for this chapter because Noritake fancy line items were often given as gifts on special occasions. We know this is so because collectors have found pieces with the original gift tags (C.154, above, is an instance, although the Christmas gift tag found with that set is not shown; other examples were shown and discussed in my first book, pp.16–17; 24). The items shown in this chapter are distinctive, however, in being decorated *specifically* for use as gifts for identified special occasions. The items in other chapters, by and large, are what might be thought of as "general purpose" special occasion items.

There are, though, exceptions to even these seemingly simple principles. For example, the decoration on a very unusual tumbler shown in Chapter T indicates fairly clearly that it was intended for use by golfers—e.g., at a club's "19th hole." One can also imagine such cups being awarded to a golfer who won an important round or who was fortunate enough to have made a hole-in-one. On such grounds, one could argue that this tumbler or cup should have been included in this chapter. Another example, again in this book, is F.33—a figurine in the form of a jeep-like vehicle. The markings around the backstamp lend support to the hypothesis that the piece may have been used at some sort of special occasion sponsored in some way by the Toyota Company. Lacking any *clear* indication that this was the case, however, it was placed in Chapter F: Figurines.

An even more flagrant violation of the views expressed above is an item which in fact does have words on the bottom that indicate quite clearly it was used at a specific special occasion: a New Year's Eve party at the Hotel McAlpin. Although such an item clearly could have been included in this chapter, it was not because most collectors and dealers think of it primarily as a covered box and so it is shown as item B.310 in Chapter B: Bowls and Boxes. A similar story explains why the cat-kitten figurine (F.31) is shown in Chap-

ter F, rather than in this chapter, even though markings on the bottom make it quite clear it was intended as a Mother's Day gift.

I give these examples in part because of the way they help me to explain how difficult it was to decide where to put the first item (H.3, shown below).

H.3 Frank Frisch memento. 2.5"h x 5.75"w x 4.75"d. Backstamp: 07.0 (46755). $400+

Before making my admittedly debatable decision to place it in this chapter, I seriously considered putting H.3 in Chapters A (Ashtrays, etc.), F (Figurines) and Z (Miscellaneous). Although some think the piece is an ashtray, this is by no means clear-cut and obvious, so I rejected Chapter A. Others think it is an unusual figurine and, thus, that it should be in Chapter F. This view may, of course, prove to be correct but, since the piece might have been an ashtray *and* few if any "figurines" have utilitarian purposes, I ultimately rejected the suggestion that it should be in Chapter F. At this point, it was tempting to dodge the question and put the piece in Chapter Z, but this was rejected because the piece has the name "Frank Frisch" written on it. To me, and to some others, this has pointed to the *possibility* that the piece was used at or for some special occasion involving this Hall of Fame baseball player.

Indeed, it has been suggested, but not yet proven, that this very unusual Noritake item was a "party favor" given to those who attended a banquet (in Japan? The backstamp is one normally used on pieces intended for the domestic market; see Table 3.1, Chapter 3) honoring Mr. Frisch for having been inducted, in 1947, into the Baseball Hall of Fame. If true, this "fact," besides being of general interest, would then also be of interest for the way it lends support to yet another interesting but as yet unsubstantiated claim—namely, that the first two digits of the five digit numbers found in some Noritake backstamps (e.g., on many of the dresser dolls and powder boxes shown in Chapter D) indicate the year (of the twentieth century) when the design of a piece was registered.

In this case (see backstamp information at the end of caption H.3), the first two numerals (4 and 6) of the design number (46755) would indicate that the piece was designed or registered in 1946. Mr. Frisch, however, was elected to the Baseball Hall of Fame in 1947. Those skeptical of the theory about the design numbers would at this point consider the case closed. Others, however, would note that his induction probably had been anticipated for some time. Since some months or even a year might be required to design and produce such a piece for use at some sort of occasion marking this event, it can be said (though not without question) that this supports the hypothesis that the first two numerals of design numbers incorporated into Noritake backstamps indicate the (twentieth century) year the design was completed or registered.

This is, I must stress, merely a hypothesis at this point; the near convergence of the first two numerals in the backstamp with the Frisch induction year could be totally coincidental. Nevertheless, other cases that fit the hypothesis are far from rare. For example, the first two numerals of those cigarette jars, dresser dolls and powder boxes which have such design numbers at all are nearly always 2 (indicating the 1920s) and most if not all are 5 or higher, a fact consistent with the Art Deco character of these items. There are counter examples, however. Consider, in this regard, the cake plate shown in P.143. It has a rather Deco or at least a 1920s look and yet the design number on this piece is 37525. Given the above hypothesis, one would have to say that the design was registered in 1937—a year many would think of as late for such a design. Obviously, to settle a matter such as this one, we need more cases or, better still, information from the Noritake Company.

Other than the very puzzling but equally dazzling ball glove piece, the other eight items of this chapter all pertain to Father's and Mother's Days. These are fine examples of some of the many Noritake holiday and special occasion (or "Limited Edition") items that were and still are made, usually in successive years (e.g., Valentine Hearts, Christmas Bells and Easter Eggs—the latter being the only one of these three still being made). The years are almost always shown on these items. Knowing nothing else, it might seem reasonable to conclude that the eight items shown in this chapter constitute two complete sets. They have the same years and are unbroken runs.

As nice as it would be if it were true, in fact, it happens that one of these sets is incomplete. If you like, you can do the detective work yourself since the information you need is in the captions in this chapter. (If you do want to do this, stop reading this paragraph now and, instead, look at the captions. If you prefer to be told why, then read on.)

We begin by considering the 1974 Father's Day mug or old-fashioned glass shown in H.5. There, the caption states that one will find, on the piece, the words "Third Edition, One of 2,500," along with backstamp 70.7. Not everyone knows, I have learned, that the words "Third Edition" on Noritake pieces mean that the item in question is the third one of a series. Since H.5 is only the second piece shown, it must be presumed that some sort of Father's Day mug or old-fashioned glass—or *something* that began the series—was produced in 1972. This must be so since it is the only way for the 1974 item to be the "Third Edition"—i.e., the third in a series. The Noritake Easter Eggs also illustrate this. The series began in 1971 and the 1998 egg is, correctly given the rule being discussed here, the "Twenty-Eighth Edition."

In contrast to the hypothesis about the baseball glove, there is another source of information about the items shown in this chapter that substantiates the claims being made here regarding words like "Third Edition"—namely, Lou Ann Donahue's pioneering (but unfortunately out of print) book on Noritake collectibles (see *bibliography*). In it, she shows (after p.64) the 1972 Father's Day old-fashioned glass (which is porcelain in spite of the name)—a beautiful piece with a design called "Rope." She reports (p.63) that 10,000 of these were made and that they sold, originally, for $18. The 1973 design, known as "Leaves" (see H.4, below), also sold for $18 but only 9,000 were made. For the already discussed 1974 (Third) edition, both the original selling price ($17) and the quantity (2,500) dropped, a trend that continued for the quantity of the 1975 piece, "Court Cards" (1000), but not the original selling price (it was back up to $18). The last of the series was called "Fish-Trout." It sold for $20, originally, and only 400 were produced. These production figures do, by the way, have a bearing on the values of such items.

The data available to me for the Mother's Day old-fashioned glasses included edition information only on the 1976 piece (H.11), which, in addition to the backstamp, has the words "Fourth Edition, One of 500"). If accurate, what this would mean is that the Mother's Day series should have begun in 1973. This is a bit puzzling, however, since the Father's Day series began in 1972 and the 1976 old-fashioned glass was the Fifth Edition of it. Once again, Donahue comes to our rescue. She states (p.62) that the first edition of the Mother's Day series (shown here in H.8) was 1973. That item, called "Birds," originally sold for $15 and 6,000 were made. The next year, "Yellow Flowers" was issued, for $17 and in the same quantity (6,000). Although the price stayed the same in 1975 for "Pink Carnations," the production had dropped to 1,300. The downward production trend continued in 1976, with only 500 "Blue and Yellow Flowers" having been made (although Donahue's book puts the figure at 400). Again, these production figures do have a bearing on the values of such items.

Finally, I offer a brief explanation for why the first item shown in this chapter has such a low caption number (H.3). As in the other chapters of this book, the first item in this chapter does begin with the next number after the last numbered caption in the same chapter of my first book on Noritake collectibles. Although 35 examples of two kinds of items (25 Easter Eggs and 10 Valentine Hearts) were shown in Chapter H of that book, only two of them were actually given numbered captions; hence the use of the number 3 to designate the first Chapter H item in this book.

H.6 Cup, Father's Day 1975. 3.25"h x 3.38"w. Backstamp: 70.07 (Fourth edition, 1 of 1000). $100-150.

H.4 Cup, Father's Day 1973. 3.38"h x 3.88"w. Backstamp: 66.57. $120-170.

H.7 Cup, Father's Day 1976. 3.25"h x 3.38"w. Backstamp: 70.07 (Fifth edition, 1 of 500). $180-200.

H.5 Cup, Father's Day 1974. 3.25"h x 3.38"w. Backstamp: 70.07 (Third edition, 1 of 2,500). $100-150.

H.8 Cup, Mother's Day 1973. 3.25"h x 3.5"w.
Backstamp: 66.57. $100-150.

H.10 Cup, Mother's Day 1975. 3.25"h x 3.38"w.
Backstamp: 70.07. $100-150.

H.9 Cup, Mother's Day 1974. 3.25"h x 3.5"w.
Backstamp: 66.57. $100-150.

H.11 Cup, Mother's Day 1976. 3.25"h x
3.38"w. Backstamp: 70.07 (Fourth edition,
1 of 500). $180-200.

Chapter L

Lamps, Night Lights, and Candleholders

In this chapter are photos showing Noritake porcelains that were, in one way or another and to be precise about it, *parts* of lights of some kind. That is, none of these items were lights in and of themselves. Rather, in order to be lights they all need an additional something, such as candles and bulbs most basically, plus quite a variety of other things including, for example, a power source such as a match or electricity as well as switches, power cords and a whole lot more. As such, these items are unlike most if not all of the other items shown in this book.

The items shown in this chapter are clustered into two unlabeled subgroups: those that need candles in order to be lights and those that need bulbs. Within each of those tacit subgroups, the items are sorted into two alphabetically sequenced sets, as follow:

Candlesticks (pp.117-118)
Chambersticks (pp.118-119)
Lamp, centerpiece (p.120)
Night lights (pp.120-121)

None of the items shown in this chapter could be called commonplace. Indeed, it is surprising, I think, how hard it is to find good *pairs* of candlesticks. A few of the items shown here, however, are not just uncommon. Rather, they are among the rarest and most spectacular items in the entire book. Three are particularly noteworthy in this regard: the center piece lamp, L.35, which gives a simply wonderful warm glow when lit, and the two night lights, L.36 and L.37. The rarity, on the collectibles market, of two-piece 1920s Noritake porcelain night lights may be explained, at least in part, by two factors. First, many of these lamps must have been broken accidentally over the years. There are several reasons for this. Children, who often were insufficiently aware of the fragility of porcelain, used most of these porcelain night lights. Moreover, the top half of most Noritake night lights are tall and, thus, can easily be knocked over. In addition, the typical upper piece simply rests on the bottom half of the lamp without a device to fasten the two pieces together. Second and in view of what was just said, those few two-piece Noritake porcelain night lights from the 1920s that have survived become treasured heirlooms that few families give up easily.

L.23 Candlesticks. 9.25"h x 4.5"w. Backstamp: 27.0. Each, $100-130.

L.24 Candlesticks. 9.0"h x 4.38"w. Backstamp: 27.0. Each, $100-130.

L.25 Candlesticks. 8.25"h x 4.88"w.
Backstamp: 27.0. Each, $120-160.

L.28 Candlesticks. 2.5"h x 5.38"w. Backstamp: 27.1. Each, $80-100.

L.26 Candlesticks. 5.25"h x 3.75"w. Backstamp: 27.1.
Each, $80-100.

L.29 Chambersticks. 3.0"h x 4.75"w. Backstamp: 27.0. Each,
$100-130.

L.27 Candlesticks. 3.75"h x 4.25"w. Backstamp: 27.0. Each, $90-110.

L.30 Chambersticks. 2.75"h x 4.38"w. *Left*, Backstamp: 27.0; *Right*, Backstamp: 27.1. Each, $100-130.

L.31 Chambersticks. 1.88"h x 5.25"w. Backstamp: 27.1. Each, $110-140.

L.32 Chambersticks. 2.0"h x 4.38"w. Backstamp: 27.0. Each, $60-70.

L.33 Chambersticks. 1.63"h x 2.5"w. Backstamp: 27.1. Each, $30-50.

L.34 Chambersticks. 1.63"h x 2.5"w. Backstamp: 27.1. Each, $30-50.

L.35 Centerpiece lamp. 6.5"h x
9.25"w. Backstamp: 27.0. $1700+

L.35A Lamp in L35 illuminated. The metal base of this lamp is
7.5"dia.

L.36B Detail of L36.

L.36 Night light.12.25"h x 4.88"w.
Backstamp: 27.0. $1800+

L.36A Back view of night
light in L.36.

L.37 Night light. 7.75"h x 4.0"w. Backstamp: 29.0 (25920). $1500+

L.37B Detail of lamp in L.37.

L.37A Lamp in L37 illuminated. The face is relatively dark because the porcelain in the heads of such pieces normally is much thicker, thus letting less light through.

Chapter P

Plaques, Plates, Trays, and Other Flat Items

In this chapter, the many plates, plaques, trays, serving plates and other basically flat items shown in it are grouped as follows:

This lengthy list gives the impression that there are many kinds of plates and, in fact, there are. Even so, it can just as well be said that, when it comes to Noritake fancy line plates, there are, in a sense, just two kinds: (1) small lemon plates and (2) all the other plates, trays, and plaques which are quite large by comparison. I have always looked forward to taking pictures of large plates, plaques and trays because there nearly always are, potentially at least, several powerful small pictures within the overall motif. I find it interesting and pleasurable to search for these. More often than I wish, the curve of a piece or a bit of glare spoils the results but now and then the picture that emerges can almost take your breath away with its intimacy and holding power. I have long advocated taking the time to look closely at the motifs on Noritake porcelains because there almost always is a lot more to savor than one can see from the usual viewing distance. For most people, this is usually about 18 inches but, to get the effect I am trying to describe, it should be more like 6 inches or even less.

I believe the close-ups of the eight cake plates at the outset of this chapter clearly show the payoff in the approach to seeing that I am advocating here. Any one of these plates is impressive enough when seen from the usual viewing distance or even from half-a-dozen feet away. Seen up close, however, they do wonderful things for all but the most hardened soul. They can encourage us to dream and

imagine and ponder; they can make us smile and marvel and wonder. What more could one possibly want from a 70-year-old piece of painted porcelain?

At the start of Chapter B, I commented at some length on items with the so-called "Deco cottage" motif. Cake plate P.139 should be considered in light of those remarks. It is an exceptional example of the type, although one might argue this motif should be called a "Deco mansion" rather than cottage. The house itself is stylized but has few truly exaggerated components. If anything, the tone is nostalgic, though certainly not in the way that Tree-in-the-Meadow items are. A major part of the difference, and of the grounds for considering pieces with motifs like this one to be Deco, is the way the flowers and trees have been done, both their forms and colors. They are anything but realistic; they are dramatic, to say the very least.

Were there a Noritake "bang for your buck" prize, lemon plates would win hands down. Those shown in this chapter should be sufficient proof, if more were needed after the more than 50 shown in my first Noritake book. This time, there are "only" 14. All are excellent and many are miniature Deco masterpieces, nearly all of them florals. Consider, for example, the delightful motif on P.154. The flower itself nicely balances realism (e.g., in the colors) with stylization (e.g., in the impossibly thin and dramatically curved stem). It is the background, however, that moves this piece from good to unusually strong. Although deceptively simple, it deftly pulls your imagination into the distance at the same time that the flower is practically "in your face" close. Regarding the floral motif on P.158, however, I am not confident in saying that it is Deco. I do know that it is one of *the* most powerful floral designs in this chapter and that many collectors of Deco Noritake would love having anything with this motif. Interestingly, this is one of the few, if not the only, lemon plates that fully incorporates the side-handle into the design. Since it is so satisfying, one wonders why this was not done more often. Another unusual motif, whether for lemon or any other plates, or indeed, any other Noritake, is the checked motif in P.165.

Surprisingly, there do not appear to be all that many round handle-less Noritake plates that are not parts of sets. The few included in this chapter, however, make up in quality for the lack of quantity. Most unusual, I think, is the plate (P.175) with an elegantly dressed woman looking over the remains of what appears to have been a fancy masquerade ball—an event far more common in the 1920s than at present. Only with the close look provided in P.175A, however, can we easily see that she appears to be savoring a glass of champagne while contemplating ... what? The clean up task that awaits her? Or, if not that, then you tell me!

Noritake collectors can be divided into various groups depending on their collecting preferences and, often, the boundaries are quite clear (and friendly). Thus, there are those who can't imagine why anyone would want wacky designs of the sort on P.178 and P.179; for others, the reaction is the opposite—they can't get enough of them. I'll leave it to you to guess where I put myself. In my experience, collectors of Deco Noritake generally find weird and wacky items appealing. This being the case, one may predict that readers with an interest in Art Deco would be drawn strongly to these two plates, as well as to the one shown in P.180. That one has qualities that make it seem a lot like drawings made famous by Dr. Seuss (who has probably never before been referenced in the context of a discussion of Art Deco).

Up to now, all center-handled Noritake serving plates of which I have been aware were either round or somewhat squared off. If that is your experience too, you will want to take note of the *oval* center-handled plate in P.191. If you are still trying to get a handle on what makes a floral motif Art Deco, then you will want to consider the plate shown in P.186, also. There's that unusual green, again, and the use of dark lines to beef up, by 1920s standards, the otherwise realistic floral elements around the edge. A great Deco vase with this same motif is shown in V.195. And if that doesn't clinch it, the tray in P.195 is all but guaranteed to settle the matter. Bold, unreal colors in the flowers, speed stripes swishing through the center, strongly contrasting free-form but yet controlled zones of color—Noritake florals do not come any more Deco than this.

Again, not all the outstanding pieces in this chapter have been mentioned and not all of them have Art Deco motifs. They all do need to be given a close look, however, so you may as well get started.

P.137 Cake plate. 1.0"h x 10.5"w x 9.75"d. Backstamp: 27.1. $290-340.

P.137A Detail of P.137.

P.138A Detail of
P.138.

P.138 Cake plate. 1.0"h x 10.5"w x 9.75"d.
Backstamp: 27.1. $290-340.

P.139 Cake plate. 1.0"h x 10.5"w x
10.0"d. Backstamp: 27.1. $140-160.

P.139A Detail of P.139.

P.140 Cake plate. 1.25"h x 9.75"w x 9.25"d. Backstamp: 16.0.
$120-150.

P.140A Detail of P.140.

P.141 Cake plate. 1.0"h x 10.0"w x 9.0"d. Backstamp: 27.1. $140-170.

P.141A Detail of P.141.

P.142 Cake plate. 1.0"h x 10.0"w x 9.0"d.
Backstamp: 25.1. $140-170.

P.142A Detail of P.142.

P.143 Cake plate. 2.0"h x 9.5"w x 8.75"d. Backstamp:
29.1 (37525). $290-330.

P.143A Detail of P.143.

P.144 Cake plate. 1.05"h x 8.75"w x 8.75"d. Backstamp: 29.1. $100-120.

P.144A Detail of P.144.

P.145 Child's plate and cup. Plate, .75"h x 7.25"dia. Cup, 2.63"h x 3.63"w. Backstamp: 27.1. $200-260.

P.145A Detail of P.145.

P.146 Chip and dip set (one piece). 2.5"h x 9.0"w.
Backstamp: 27.0. $80-110.

P.148 Multi-piece serving set. 1.5"h x 8.25"dia.
Backstamp: 27.0. $150-170.

P.147 Multi-piece serving set. 1.25"h x 11.75"dia.
Backstamp: 27.0. $100-140.

P.149 Multi-piece serving set. 3.88"h x 10.0"dia.
Backstamp (all pieces are marked): 27.1. $160-190.

P.150 Multi-piece serving (sweetmeat) set. Box, 1.63"h x 9.38"dia. Center dish, .88"h x 4.0"dia. Backstamp: 27.0. $280-330.

P.150A Detail of P.150.

P.152 Multi-piece (asparagus) serving set. Plate, 1.5"h x 12.0"w. x 9.5"d. Sauce bowl, 3.0"h x 6.5"d. x 3.13"d. Backstamp: 27.1. $160-190.

P.151 Multi-piece (tiered) serving set. Overall, 9.5"h. Upper plate, 7.75"dia. Lower plate, 10.25"dia. Backstamp: 27.1. $70-100.

P.153 Ice cream set. Serving tray, .88"h x 12.75"d. x 7.5"d. Individual plate, .63"h x 5.5"w. Backstamp: 27.0. $220-300.

P.156 Round, side-handled lemon plate. 1.25"h x 6.38"dia. Backstamp: 27.1. $40-60.

P.154 Round, side-handled lemon plate. 1.5"h x 6.5"dia. Backstamp: 27.1. $60-80.

P.155 Round, side-handled lemon plate. 1.5"h x 6.5"dia. Backstamp: 27.1. $60-80.

P.159 Round, side-handled lemon plate. 1.25"h x 5.63"dia. Backstamp: 25.1. $40-60.

P.157 Round, side-handled lemon plate. 1.25"h x 6.38"dia. Backstamp: 27.1. $40-60.

P.160 Round, side-handled lemon plate. 1.25"h x 5.5"dia. Backstamp: 27.1. $60-80.

P.158 Round, side-handled lemon plate. 1.5"h x 6.25"dia. Backstamp: 27.1. $70-90.

P.161 Round, side-handled lemon plate. 1.25"h x 5.5"dia. Backstamp: 26.1. $60-80.

P.162 Round, side-handled lemon plate. 1.25"h x 5.5"dia. Backstamp: 27.1. $30-50.

P.164 Round, solid center-handled lemon plate. 2.0"h x 5.75"dia. Backstamp: 25.1. $50-70.

P.163 Round, side-handled lemon plate. 1.25"h x 5.5"dia. Backstamp: 27.1. $30-50.

P.165 Round, loop center-handled lemon plate. 2.5"h x 5.25"dia. Backstamp: 27.1. $80-90.

P.166 Round, loop center-handled lemon plate. 2.5"h x 6.75"dia. Backstamp: 27.1. $50-80.

P.167 Round, loop center-handled lemon plate. 2.5"h x 6.75"dia. Backstamp: 27.1. $50-80.

P.169 Sided, butterfly-handled lemon plate. 1.5"h x 6.25"dia. Backstamp: 27.1. $70-90.

P.168 Round, loop center-handled lemon plate. 2.5"h x 6.75"dia. Backstamp: 19.2. $40-60.

P.170 Sided, butterfly-handled lemon plate. 1.5"h x 6.25"dia. Backstamp: 27.1. $70-90.

P.171 Plaque. 1.13"h x 10.63"dia. Backstamp: 76.3. $140-180.

P.171A Detail of P.171.

P.172 Plaque. 1.38"h x 10.13"dia. Backstamp: 27.0. $160-200.

P.172A Detail of P.172.

P.173 Plaque. 1.0"h x
8.25"dia. Backstamp: 77.3.
$130-150.

P.173A Detail of P.173.

P.174 Plaque. .88"h x 6.25"dia.
Backstamp: 25.1. $180-230.

P.176 Plate. 1.5"h x 8.63"dia. Backstamp: 16.7. $200-250.

P.175 Plate. 1.25"h x 8.75"dia. Backstamp:
27.1. $350-390.

P.175A Detail of P.175.

P.177 Plate. 1.25"h x 7.63"dia. Backstamp: 14.0. $110-140.

P.179 Plate. 1.0"h x 8.75"dia. Backstamp: 27.0. $100-130.

P.178 Plate. .63"h x 6.25"dia. Backstamp: 27.0. $170-220.

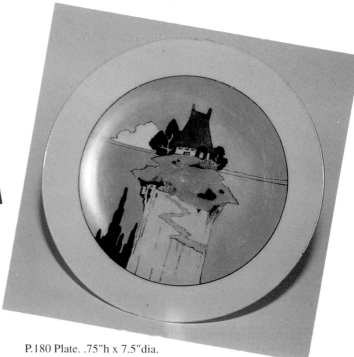

P.180 Plate. .75"h x 7.5"dia. Backstamp: 27.0. $120-160.

P.181 Plate with two handles. .88"h x 7.75"w. x 7.25"d. Backstamp: 27.1. $60-80.

P.182 Plate with two handles. .88"h x 7.75"w. x 7.25"d. Backstamp: 27.1. $50-70.

P.183 Plate with two handles. .75"h x 7.75"w. x 7.25"d. Backstamp: 27.1. $60-80.

P.184 Sandwich plate. 3.25"h x 9.5"w. Backstamp: 27.1.
$100-130.

P.186 Sandwich plate. 3.75"h x 9.38"w. Backstamp: 27.1.
$130-180.

P.185 Sandwich plate. 3.25"h x 8.0"w.
Backstamp: 27.1. $90-140.

P.187 Sandwich plate. 3.75"h x
10.0"dia. Backstamp: 27.1. $90-130.

P.188 Sandwich plates. 3.25"h x 9.5"dia. Backstamp: 27.0. Each, $270-310.

P.188A Detail of P.188, *Left*.

P.188B Detail of P.188, *Right*.

P.189 Sandwich plate. 3.75"h x
9.75"dia. Backstamp: 27.1. $100-150.

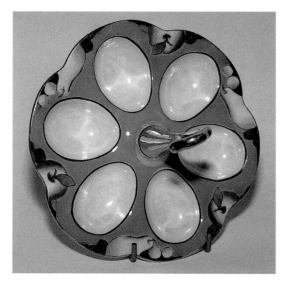

P.190 Center handled serving plate for eggs. 4.5"h x
6.5"w. Backstamp: 27.0. $90-130.

P.191. Serving plate. 4.5"h x 11.5 w x 8.5 d. Backstamp: 27.1.
$80-110.

P.193 Serving plate. 2.0"h x 7.0"w x 5.75"d. Backstamp: 27.1.
$100-130.

P.192 Serving plate. 2.0"h x 7.0"w x 5.75"d.
Backstamp: 27.1. $80-110.

P.194 Tray. 1.13"h x 11.75"dia. Backstamp: 27.0. $130-160.

P.195 Tray. 1.25"h x 10.88"w. x 8.38"d. Backstamp: 27.1. $190-240.

P 195A Detail of P 195

P.196 Tray. 1.25"h x 10.88"w
x 8.38"d. Backstamp: 27.1.
$190-240.

P.196A Detail of P.196.

P.197 Tray. 1.25"h x 10.88"w. x 8.38"d. Backstamp: 27.1.
$190-240.

P.197A Detail of P.197.

Chapter S
Salesman Sample Pages and Other Paper Items

In a book about porcelains this chapter is somewhat unconventional, since the materials shown in it are made of paper. It is relevant because all these materials can be linked to Noritake porcelains in some fairly direct way. In my first book on Noritake porcelains, materials like those shown in this chapter were discussed in Part One (on p.16 of Chapter 2) and shown on pp.19–23. Such materials are rare, visually interesting and of considerable importance to Noritake collectors and dealers.

There are two kinds of paper materials in this chapter. All but one of the items shown are "salesman sample book pages." In North America, these pages are rare or, to be more precise, collectors of Noritake own few. Therefore, I am particularly pleased to thank Mr. Fred Tenney and Dr. and Mrs. Dennis Buonafede for allowing me to photograph these and other pages in their collections and for agreeing to have them included in this and my previous Noritake book. (I have no idea how many are owned by collectors of paper.) Prior to World War II, sales personnel working on behalf of the Noritake Company carried around thick loose-leaf notebooks full of pages like these to show prospective customers what could be ordered. Salesmen added and deleted pages as the possibilities changed.

These pages, which typically were 11.5" high and 7.5" wide overall, were not printed. Rather, each page was an individually painted, original work of art. This is important and impressive to the collector today, but not all that surprising, given the time period we are talking about (1900–1930) and the fact that the Noritake Company obviously would have had scores if not hundreds of skilled artists available to produce them. Even if we assume, as seems reasonable, that scores of books were needed, we may speculate that it would not have been too difficult to produce them, since many of the Noritake Company artists would have been capable of painting a page like the ones we see in this chapter in only a few minutes. This, I think, is at least part of the fascination with these materials, though it is by no means the main one.

Another fascination is being able to match a page to a piece. Usually one is limited to doing this by comparing pages to photos of pieces or photos of pages to actual pieces. In some instances, when we do this, we discover that there are salesmen's sample pages for which no corresponding piece of Noritake porcelain is yet known. One thus is given the basis for hoping that, in the not too distant future, the unknown piece will turn up at an antique show— when *we* are there. Sometimes, though, it is possible to bring piece and page together. When I took the photos shown in this chapter, I was able to do this for two of the pages.

S.1 Noritake salesman sample book page with matching plate. Page, 11.5"h x 7.5"w. Plate, .88"h x 6.5"dia. Backstamp 27.0. Plate, $30-50.

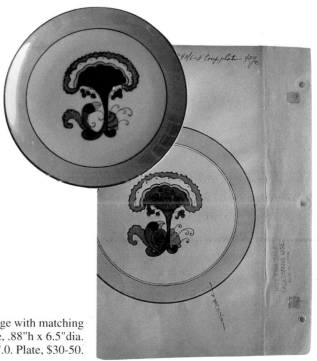

S.2 Noritake salesman sample book page with matching plate. Page, 11.5"h x 7.5"w. Plate, .88"h x 6.5"dia. Backstamp 27.0. Plate, $30-50.

The results are fascinating for several reasons. In the first place, we see that the painted pages show these two objects at full size. Most of the other pages apparently do this as well. Also, the colors are very close to those that appear on the actual pieces. This is what one would expect, of course, but in such matters, it is not something that could simply be presumed. There is something else fascinating about these two examples. The designs on the two plates are rather weird, at least by the standards of most Noritake collectors and, for that matter, by the standards of most other Noritake porcelains.

The plate with the blue rim was known before these pages were found. The motif on it was so unusual, some were reduced to speculating that *maybe* it was just the product of a Noritake artist's whim one day. Although nobody I know of took this idea all that seriously, I mention it to indicate how very puzzling this motif seemed. With this in mind, then, it should not be difficult to imagine that finding these particular salesman sample book pages was a fairly interesting moment for many Noritake collectors (amazingly, the yellow-rimmed plate was found a few days before these photos were taken).

As the full title of this chapter indicates, the materials relevant to it are not limited to salesman sample pages. There are other paper items that are of direct interest and relevance to Noritake collectors. Examples of such paper items were discussed in my first Noritake book, again, in Chapter 2 (see p.11). They also were shown, by means of the wonderful photos by Margaret Anderson Hetzler comparing motifs on Noritake porcelains with similar motifs found on

other items from the 1920s such as playing cards and bridge tally sets (see photos 2.11, 2.12, 2.13, and 2.14). Had those photos not been published already, they could have been included in this chapter.

There is, however, one such photograph in this chapter (see Photo S.3). It is, I believe, a rather important one. It shows the cover of a French magazine from the 1920s. The title of the magazine, *Le Soirire*, translates as "The Smile." This issue was published on Thursday 10 February 1927. On seeing it, many experienced Noritake collectors will quickly recognize that this is a version, a much more (shall we say?) "dramatic" rendition, of a well known motif found on an oval Noritake dresser tray. One such tray is shown in Chapter D (see Photo D.129 and D.129A). The magazine cover drawing is captioned "*Une Degringoleuse De Pontes*"—a rather idiomatic phrase that translates, roughly, as "falling hot shot."

Routinely, so I am told by friends in the design field, designers today as in years past develop motifs that they consider to be their own after they have spent considerable amounts of time studying the designs of others. Such design work, which is not at all the same as *directly* copying a design to the last tiny detail (something that *is* frowned upon), is apparently all part of the game, or at least that is what I am told. I mention this because I know that some Noritake collectors worry that showing examples of non-Noritake designs that converge with Noritake motifs might have the unintended effect of casting the pre-World War II New York Noritake design department in a bad light. I, however, am not so sure this will happen, and it certainly shouldn't. Instead, showing photos such as this one will have at least two benefits. First, it will inform collectors about the spread and history of designs that are important to them. Second, it should foster among them an interest in an as yet poorly developed collecting area—namely, the search for examples of designs that are similar to those found on Noritake porcelains. In all of this, of course, it will be necessary, continuously, to guard against drawing conclusions too casually as to who was inspired by whom.

S.3 Thursday, 10 February 1927 cover of the French magazine *Le Soirire*. Compare this scene to the one shown on the dresser tray in D.129 and D.129A, above (p.100). 11.0"h x 9.0"w.

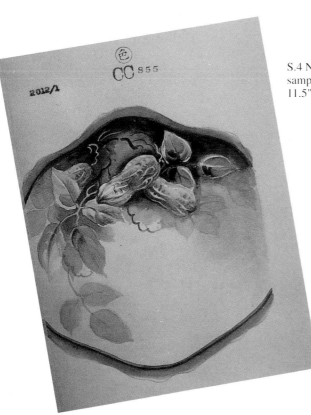

S.4 Noritake salesman sample book page. 11.5"h x 7.5"w.

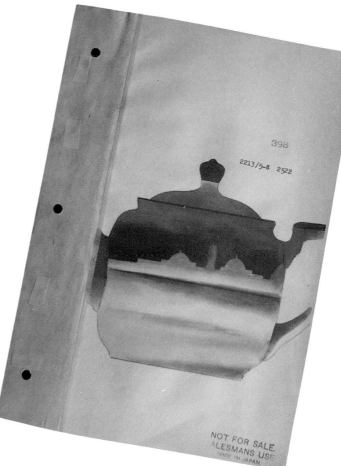

S.6 Noritake salesman sample book page. 11.5"h x 7.5"w.

S.5 Noritake salesman sample book page. 11.5"h x 7.5"w.

S.7 Noritake salesman sample book page. 11.5"h x 7.5"w.

S.8 Noritake salesman sample book page. 11.5"h x 7.5"w.

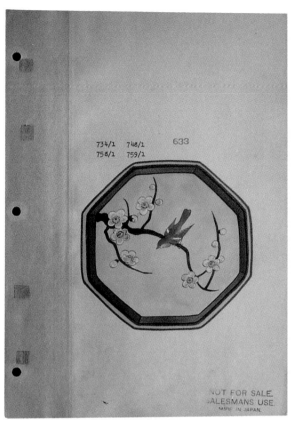

S.9 Noritake salesman sample book page. 11.5"h x 7.5"w.

S.11 Noritake salesman sample book page. 11.5"h x 7.5"w.

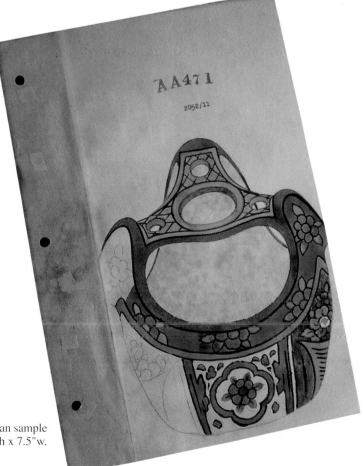

S.10 Noritake salesman sample book page. 11.5"h x 7.5"w.

S.12 Noritake salesman sample book
page. 11.5"h x 7.5"w.

S.13 Noritake salesman sample
book page. 11.5"h x 7.5"w.

S.14 Noritake
salesman sample book
page. 11.5"h x 7.5"w.

S.16 Noritake salesman
sample book page. 11.5"h
x 7.5"w.

S.15 Noritake salesman
sample book page. 11.5"h
x 7.5"w.

S.17 Noritake salesman sample book
page. 11.5"h x 7.5"w.

S.18 Noritake salesman sample book
page. 11.5"h x 7.5"w.

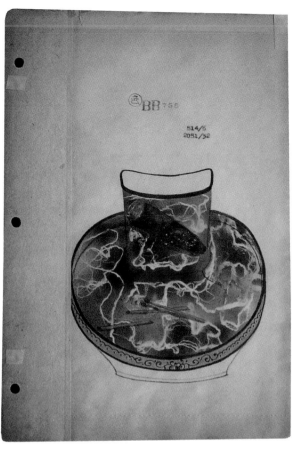

S.19 Noritake salesman sample book page. 11.5"h x 7.5"w.

S.20 Noritake salesman sample book page. 11.5"h x 7.5"w.

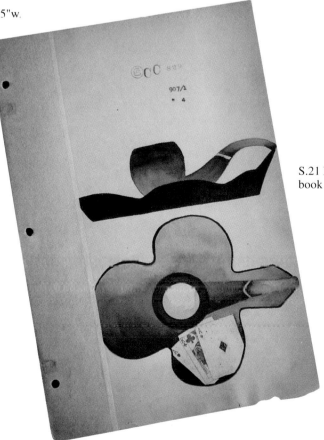

S.21 Noritake salesman sample book page. 11.5"h x 7.5"w.

Chapter T

Tea Sets and Other Items Pertaining to Beverages

Tea sets and related items are the focus of this chapter. The items shown are grouped and sequenced as follows:

Even though this chapter has quite a few sub-categories and pertains to a kind of product that the Noritake company was famous for making many varieties of, this chapter is one of the smaller ones in this book. This undoubtedly is the result of several factors, but one of them seems to be collector preference. For some reason or reasons, the Noritake collectors known to me do not have all that many beverage (tea, coffee, chocolate) sets. Be that as it may, some *outstanding* pieces are shown in this chapter.

For example, the superb breakfast sets shown in T.79 and T.80 are, in my experience, quite unusual. Finding complete sets of these cannot be easy. At least as rare is the child's tea set in its original and much used box (T.81). All the various bottles and jugs shown (T75 – T.78) are quite interesting, with both the cordial bottle and ewer being almost unprecedented. The real mystery to me, though, is the "jug" in T.75 (I pondered long and hard before settling on this less than completely satisfactory name). What is it for? What was its basic function? The "obvious" answer—that it is some sort of jug or pitcher (some say saki bottle, though that seems wrong on several counts, size being a primary one)—has never satisfied me because it is *very* difficult to pour liquid from the spout of this item without some of it spilling over the sides at the top. Regardless of its function, the decoration is exceptional, especially for those who have a penchant for floral Noritake.

One of the more dramatic items in the chapter is the chocolate set in T.84. The close up shown with it (T.84A) was taken of this motif as it appears on another item. If you look closely, you will be able to see that there are differences in the two ladies (hint: examine the flowers)—i.e., these decorations were painted *by hand*. The coffee set in T.86 is interesting because it seems so clearly to have a 1950s look. Consistent with this, the backstamp on these pieces (77.3) was registered in the mid-1950s. Interestingly, though, this backstamp was for use on items that would be sold in Japan. The demitasse sets in T.88 and T.89 could hardly differ more and yet both are spectacular, each in its own way. One is a superb example of traditional elegance and the other an equally great example of Deco-era fascination with the tropics and similar exotic places.

All of the cream and sugar sets are attention grabbing, for me, but, as was noted at length in Chapter 2, the one in T.93 is especially riveting, for those who love Deco. While you are in Chapter T, compare this motif to the one on the tea tile shown in T.105. The item labeled as a "sugar cube holder" (T.98) may be correctly named and it may not be. I asked quite a few people to say what they thought it was and this was the consensus. If you have a different view, let me know. Finally, consider the last two items of the chapter—the golf cup or tumbler in T.112 and the wine caddy in T.113. Both are unique in my experience.

And so are the tastes and preferences of every reader of this book, so don't lose sight of your opinions about the items shown in this chapter as you turn, now, to an examination of them.

T.75 Jug. 7.25"h x 4.0"w x 3.75"d.
Backstamp: 19.0. $90-130.

T.77 Cordial bottle. 10.75"h x 4.75"w.
Backstamp: 27.1. $160-180.

T.76 Pitcher. 5.63"h x 6.38"w x 4.5"d.
Backstamp: 27.0. $60-80.

T.78 Ewer. 10.0"h x 5.5"w.
Backstamp: 27.1. $180-200.

T.79 Breakfast set. Tray, 1.5"h x 10.25"w. Tea pot, 3.75"h x 5.5"w. Toast rack, 1.88"h x 3.0"w x 2.5"d. Cup, 2.5"h x 4.0"w x 3.38"d. Creamer, 2.38"h x 3.5"w. Jelly dish, 1.13"h x 2.0"w. Backstamp: 25.1. $300-400.

T.80 Breakfast set. Tray, .75"h x 12.0"w x 7.75"d. Egg cup, 3.5"h x 2.38"w. Cup, 2.0"h x 4.5"w x 3.63"d. Salt and pepper, 2.5"h x 1.5"w. Backstamp, 27.1. $250-300.

T.80A Alternate view of T.80.

T.81 Child's toy tea set, in original box. Box, 4.0"h x 1.50"w x 13.5"d. Pot, 3.5"h x 5.5"w. Sugar, 2.63"h x 3.75"w. Creamer, 2.0"h x 2.88"w. Cup, 1.563"h x 3.5"w. Saucer, .5"h x 4.63"dia. Backstamp: 26.0. Set of 6, $1000+

T.82 Child's toy tea set. Pot, 3.75"h x 5.25"w. Plate, 4.75"dia. Cup and saucer, 1.5"h x 4.5"w x 3.5"d. Backstamp: 27.0. Set of 6, $600+

T.82A Detail of T.82.

T.83 Child's toy tea set, Part I. Pot, 3.5"h x 5.5"w x 3.75"d. Sugar, 2.63"h x 4.25"w x 3.0"d. Creamer, 2.0"h x 3.25"w x 2.75"d. Cup, 1.38"h x 2.88"w x 2.38"d. Saucer, .5"h x 3.75"dia. Backstamp: 27.1. As shown, but with 6 cups and saucers, $750+

T.83A Child's toy tea set, Part II. Oval platter, .75"h x 7.25"w x 5.38"d. Covered casserole, 3.0"h x 6.0"w x 3.63"d. Individual plate, .5"h x 4.38"dia. Cake plate, .88"h x 6.25"w x 6.0"d. Gravy boat, 1.88"h x 4.75"w x 2.75"d. Backstamp: 27.1. As shown, 750+

T.84 Chocolate set. Pot, 9.0"h x 7.5"w. Saucer, 4.88"dia. Cup, 2.63"h x 3.25"w. Backstamp: 27.1 With six cups, $850-950.

T.84A Detail of a motif similar to the one on T.84.

T.85 Chocolate set. Pot, 8.75"h x 6.5"w x 3.75"d. Saucer, 5.0"dia. Cup, 2.75"h x 3.0"w x 2.25d. Backstamp: 27.0. With six cups, $350-450.

T.86 Coffee set. Pot, 7.5"h x 7.75"w x 4.38"d. Saucer, 6.38"dia. Cup, 2.75"h x 4.38"w x 3.63d. Creamer, 4.25"h x 4.0"w x 3.0"d. Sugar, 4.25"h x 3.75"w. Backstamp: 77.3. With six cups, $350-450.

T.87 Demitasse set. Tray, 1.0"h x 12.0"dia. Pot, 7.0"h x 7.25"w x 3.5"d. Saucer (which has full backstamp), 4.38"dia. Cup, 2.38"h x 2.88"w x 2.0"d. Creamer, 3.5"h x 4.25"w x 2.88"d. Sugar, 4.25"h x 5.38"w x 3.5"d. Backstamp: 25.1. With six cups, $550-650.

T.88 Demitasse set. Pot, 6.75"h x 6.63"w x 3.5"d. Saucer, 4.5"dia. Cup, 2.25"h x 2.88"w x 2.38"d. Creamer, 3.0"h x 3.5"w. Sugar, 3.5"h x 4.63"w. Backstamp: 16.2. With six cups, $550-650.

T.89 Demitasse set. Pot, 7.0"h x 6.5"w. Saucer, 4.25"dia. Cup, 2.0"h x 3.0"w. Creamer, 2.5"h x 3.5"w. Sugar, 3.5"h x 5.0"w. Backstamp: 27.0. With six cups, $550-650.

T.90 Cream and sugar set. Creamer, 3.25"h x
5.0"w x 3.5"d. Sugar, 4.5"h x 6.75"w x 4.25"d.
Backstamp: 19.1. $150-180.

T.91 Cream and sugar set. Creamer, 3.0"h x
4.38"w x 2.25"d. Sugar, 3.5"h x 5.13"w x
2.75"d. Backstamp: 25.1. $150-170.

T.92 Cream and sugar set. Creamer, 3.25"h x 4.25"w. Sugar, 4.0"h x 5.25"w. Backstamp: 27.1. $120-170.

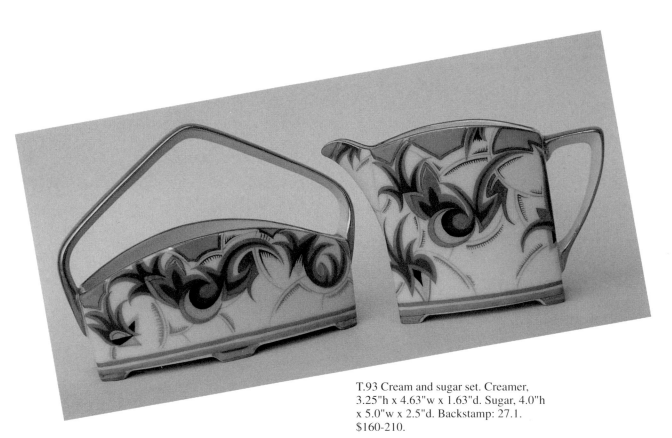

T.93 Cream and sugar set. Creamer, 3.25"h x 4.63"w x 1.63"d. Sugar, 4.0"h x 5.0"w x 2.5"d. Backstamp: 27.1. $160-210.

T.94 Cream and sugar set. Creamer, 3.38"h x 4.0"w. Sugar, 2.25"h x 6.0"w. Backstamp: 27.1. $100-150.

T.95 Cream and sugar set. Creamer, 4.0"h x 2.25"w x 2.0"d. Sugar, 3.25"h x 4.13"w x 3.0"d. Backstamp: 29.1. $90-130.

T.96 Cream and sugar set. Creamer, 3.0"h x 4.38"w x 2.25"d. Sugar, 3.38"h x 4.75"w x 3.25"d. Backstamp: 27.1. $100-140.

T.97 Cream and sugar set. Creamer, 2.38"h x
3.75"w x 2.5"d. Sugar, 3.5"h x 4.75"w x
3.25"d. Backstamp: 27.0. $90-110.

T.98 Sugar cube holder. 1.5"h x 6.88"w x 2.0"d.
Backstamp: 27.1. $140-190.

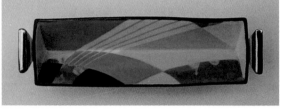

T.98A Top view of T.98.

T.99 Snack set. Tray, .88"h x 8.75"w x
7.25"d. Cup, 1.75"h x 3.38"w x 3.0"d.
Backstamp: 07.0. $70-90.

T.100 Snack set. Tray, .5"h x 9.5"w x
6.0"d. Cup, 2.0"h x 4.0"w x 3.0"d.
Backstamp: 27.1. $80-100.

T.101 Tea set. Pot, 6.0"h x 8.75"w x 5.75"d. Creamer, 4.0"h x 4.5"w x 3.75"d. Sugar, 4.75"h x 6.25"w x 4.5"d. Plate, 1.0"h x 5.63"dia. Cup, 2.0"h x 4.25"w x 3.53"d. Saucer, .75"h x 5.5"dia. Backstamp: 27.0. With six cups and plates, $650-700.

T.102 Tea set. Pot, 4.25"h x 8.5"w x 4.5"d. Saucer, 5.5"dia. Cup, 2.13"h x 4.38"w x 3.63"d. Plate, 1.0"h x 7.63"dia. Backstamp: 27.0. With six cups and plates, $450-550.

T.103 Tea strainer. Strainer, .88"h x 5.5"w x 3.75"d. Underplate, .75"h x 4.88"w. Backstamp: 27.1. $110-150.

T.104 Tea strainer. Strainer, .88"h x 5.5"w x 3.75"d. Underplate, .75"h x 4.88"w. Backstamp: 27.0. $100-130.

T.105 Tea tile. .5"h x 4.88"w. Backstamp: 27.1. $120-150.

T.108 Tea tile. .5"h x 6.0"dia. Backstamp: 27.0. $100-120.

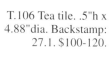

T.106 Tea tile. .5"h x 4.88"dia. Backstamp: 27.1. $100-120.

T.109 Tea tile. .5"h x 6.0"dia. Backstamp: 27.1. $110-140.

T.110 Tea tile. .5"h x 6.0"dia. Backstamp: 27.1. $130-160.

T.107 Tea tile. .5"h x 6.0"dia. Backstamp: 27.1. $120-150.

T.111 Tea tile. .5"h x 6.0"dia.
Backstamp: 27.1. $110-140.

T.111A Detail of T.111.

T.112 Tumbler. 4.5"h 3.63"w
2.25"d. Backstamp: 77.3. $90-130.

T.113 Wine caddy. 4.25"h 8.5"w 6.5"d. Backstamp: 27.0. $120-170.

T.112A Back view of
T.112.

Chapter V

Vases and Other Items Pertaining to Flowers

In this chapter there are photos of various items which, in one way or another, pertain to flowers. They are clustered into the following functional categories:

In its basic structure this chapter is organized along the same lines as the others in this book. Following the lead of Chapter B, I first group vases in terms of such features as the number of handles they have or whether they have figural elements. Within those groups, height is then used to sequence vases.These principles are simple, and result in groups that are interesting to look at.

As with the other chapters of this book, Chapter V has photos of some very special items. Some of them are fairly striking Art Deco works; others are elegant designs of a more traditional nature. Some are simply wacky or whimsical in one way or another. Here I will restrict my comments to just a dozen items. I begin, for the fun of it, with two of the "wacky-whimsical" pieces. In this department, the prize would have to go to the delightful vase in V.245 which, of all things, has a bunch of celery painted on it! The other item, which is perhaps more aptly described as charming than wacky, is the flowerpot shown in V.203. This wonderful piece is relatively rare. This is one of two that I know of, so far. Next (and this counts as just one of the items I mention here) are all four of the flower frogs shown in this chapter (V.200, V.201 and V.202). All of these must be considered rare but the Pierrot figural on the left in V.200 is, quite simply, a Noritake Art Deco masterpiece.

Art Deco works are represented throughout this chapter. Of the vases, the one that always catches and holds my eye the longest is shown here in V.235. The shade of blue is unusual and the small floral element is striking, but the gold stripes put the piece over the top, in my estimation. Another very strong Deco vase in this chapter, V.241, has the same great floral motif that we saw on the compote in B.287. The vase shown in V.244 is very unusual for Noritake, in my experience. And it feels wonderful. The entire surface is a subtle molded-in-relief and the overall shape is simple and quite elegant. The bud vases in V.250 were new to me when I saw this photograph in a huge stack of them sent to me some months ago. The floral motif on the basket vase in V.258 is quite a strong Deco design and the back of it (V.258A) nicely illustrates why these perspectives are shown in this book from time to time. That side is as strong in its own way as the front. The vase shown in V.262 and V.262A illustrates this same point. Also, as a Deco floral, it is wonderfully wacky, bold—maybe even weird—and therefore a very desirable item to many. The vase shown in V.272 is unusual in my experience but is also notable in part for having survived at all, given those very big but also quite thin handles. Last, but most assuredly not least, I turn to the wall pockets. Two of them (V.284 and V.285) are blanks that most Noritake collectors will think of as unusual if their experience is at all similar to mine. Most unusual of all, though (and without a doubt) is the one shown in V.290. This bold, amazing, rare, wonderful piece is, so far, one-of-a-kind.

Your tastes and preferences are also unique, so enough of my thoughts and reactions about the items in this chapter. What do *you* think?

V.197 Ferner. 3.0"h x 7.25"w. Backstamp: 27.0. $140-180.

V.198 Ferner. 3.75"h x 5.88"w. Backstamp: 27.0. $130-170.

V.199 Ferner. 3.63"h x 7.5"w. Backstamp: 27.0. $120-160.

V.200 Flower frogs. *Left*, 6.5"h x 3.0"w. Backstamp: 27.0. $450+ *Right*, 6.63"h x 3.75"w. Backstamp: MIJ.1. $300-350.

V.200A Back views of V.200.

V.201 Flower frog. 7.25"h
x 3.75"w. Backstamp:
27.0. $250-300.

V.202 Flower frog.
6.5"h x 2.88"w.
Backstamp: 27.1.
$260-290.

V.201A Detail of V.201.

V.203 Flower pot (2 pieces). 4.75"h x
5.0"w. Backstamp (both pieces): 27.1.
$180-200.

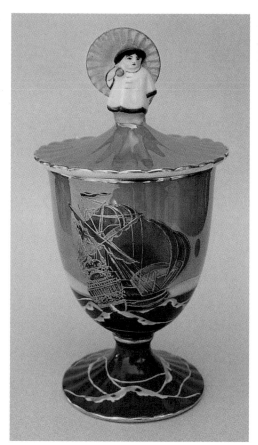

V.206 Urn. 8.75"h x
4.38"w. Backstamp:
27.0. $290-330.

V.204 Potpourri. 3.63"h x 5.38"w.
Backstamp: 27.0. $80-110.

V.207 Urn. 9.25"h x
4.25"w. Backstamp: 27.1.
$280-320.

V.205 Urns, positioned to show front and back. 11.88"h x 6.13"w x
4.38"d. Backstamp: 25.1. Each, $210-260.

V.207A Back view
of V.207.

V.210 Figural vase. 7.0"h
x 7.0"w. Backstamp:
27.0. $250-300.

V.211 Figural vase.
7.0"h x 5.5"w x
2.5"d. Backstamp:
27.0. $220-270.

V.208 Urn. 9.25"h x 4.25"w. Backstamp:
27.0. $90-130.

Vases

V.209 Figural
vase. 9.25"h x
6.5"w x 3.75"d.
Backstamp: 27.0.
$230-280.

V.211A Back
view of V.211.

V.212 Figural vases. 7.0"h x 5.5"w x 2.5"d. *Front left*, Backstamp 19.2. *Others*, Backstamp: 27.0. Each, $200-230.

V.213 Figural vase. 7.0"h x 5.5"w x 2.5"d. Backstamp: 27.0. $200-230.

V.214 Figural vase. 5.5"h x 5.0"w x 2.75"d. Backstamp: 19.1. $190-210.

V.213A Back view of V.213.

V.214A Side view of V.214.

V.215 Figural vases. 5.13"h x 3.5"w x 3.0"d. *Left*, Backstamp: 27.1. $130-170. *Right*, Backstamp: 27.0. $110-140.

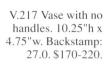

V.217 Vase with no handles. 10.25"h x 4.75"w. Backstamp: 27.0. $170-220.

V.216 Figural vase. 5.0"h x 3.5"w. Backstamp: 19.0. $120-150.

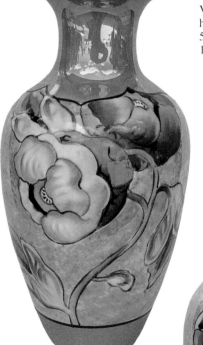

V.218 Vase with no handles. 10.0"h x 5.25"w. Backstamp: 19.1. $180-220.

V.218A Reverse of V.218.

V.221 Vases with no handles. 9.13"h x 2.63"w. Backstamp: 67.019. Each, $90-120.

V.219 Vase with no handles. 9.88"h x 5.0"w. Backstamp: 65.019. $130-160.

V.222 Vase with no handles. 9.0"h x 4.0"w. Backstamp: 19.1. $150-190.

V.220 Vase with no handles. 9.38"h x 5.0"w. Backstamp: 27.1. $380-430.

V.223 Vase with no handles. 8.75"h x 6.0"w
x 4.75"d. Backstamp: 27.0. $280-330.

V.225 Vase with no handles. 8.5"h x
3.0"w. Backstamp: 29.1 (29812).
$430-480.

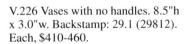

V.226 Vases with no handles. 8.5"h
x 3.0"w. Backstamp: 29.1 (29812).
Each, $410-460.

V.224 Vases with no
handles, arranged to
show front and back.
8.5"h x 6.0"w.
Backstamp: 27.0. Each,
$130-170.

V.227 Vase with no handles. 8.5"h x 3.75"w. Backstamp: 27.1. $140-160.

V.228 Vase with no handles. 8.5"h x 3.75"w. Backstamp: 27.0. $140-160.

V.230 Vase with no handles. 7.63"h x 3.5"w. Backstamp: 27.1. $200-240.

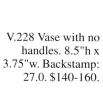

V.229 Vase with no handles. 8.13"h x 4.63"w. Backstamp: 27.0. $180-210.

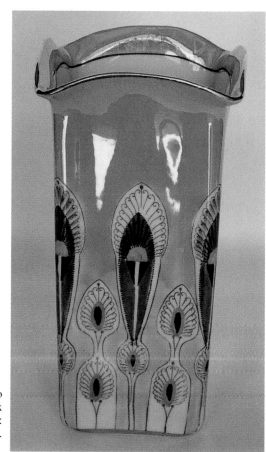

V.231 Vase with no handles. 7.63"h x 3.5"w. Backstamp: 27.1. $200-240.

V.232 Vase with no handles.
7.5"h x 3.38"w. Backstamp:
27.1. $100-150.

V.234 Vase with no handles. 7.13"h x 3.0"w.
Backstamp: 27.1. $190-230.

V.233 Vases with no handles. 7.5"h x 3.38"w. Backstamps: *Left*, 27.1; *Center*,
27.0; *Right*, 19.1. *Left*, $80-100; *Center*, $300-350; *Right*, $80-100.

V.237 Vases with no handles. 6.88"h x 3.75"w. *Right* and *left*, Backstamp: 65.019. *Center*, Backstamp: 67.019. Each, $60-80.

V.235 Vase with no handles. 7.0"h x 4.5"w. Backstamp: 25.1. $260-310.

V.236 Vase with no handles. 7.0"h x 3.0"w. Backstamp: 27.1. $140-180.

V.238 Vase with no handles. 6.88"h x 3.5"w. Backstamp: 25.1. $140-180.

V.239 Vase with no handles.
6.75"h x 3.38"w. Backstamp: 25.1.
$200-250.

V.241 Vase with no handles.
6.75"h x 5.38"w. Backstamp:
27.1. $300-400.

V.240 Vase with no handles. 6.75"h x 5.38"w.
Backstamp: 27.1. $700+

V.242 Vase with no handles. 6.75"h x 5.5"w.
Backstamp: 19.1. $180-220.

V.243 Vase with no handles.
6.75"h x 5.5"w. Backstamp:
27.1. $200-250.

V.246 Vase with no handles. 6.13"h x 6.75"w x
4.63"d. Backstamp: 27.1. $280-320.

V.244 Vase with no
handles. 6.75"h x
4.5"w. Backstamp:
25.1. $250-300.

V.247 Vase with no handles. 5.75"h x
4.0"w x 1.75"d. Backstamp: 27.1.
$150-190.

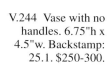

V.245 Vase with no handles.
6.75"h x 6.5"w x 4.0"d.
Backstamp: 27.1. $100-150.

V.248 Vase with no
handles. 5.63"h x 4.0"w x
1.75"d. Backstamp: 25.1.
$150-190.

V.249 Vase with no handles.
5.38"h x 5.25"w x 2.25"d.
Backstamp: 27.1. $90-130.

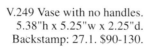

V.250 Vases with no handles. 5.0"h x 2.0"w.
Backstamp: 27.0. Each, $80-100.

V.251 Vases with no handles. 5.0"h x 3.0"w. *Left* and *right*, Backstamp, 27.1. $100-140. *Center*, Backstamp: 29.1. $90-120.

V.252 Vase with no handles. 4.5"h x 3.75"w x 2.5"d. Backstamp: 27.1. $90-130.

V.253 Vase with no handles. 4.5"h x 2.5"w. Backstamp: 27.0. $90-110.

V.254 Vases with no handles. 4.0"h x 2.5"w x 2.5"d. Backstamp: 67.019. Each, $50-60.

V.256 Vase with one handle. 10.0"h x 6.25"w. Backstamp: 27.1. $400-450.

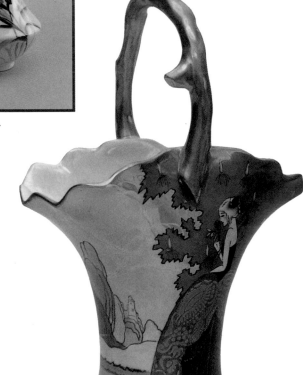

V.255 Vase with one handle. 9.0"h x 5.0"w. Backstamp: 25.1. $170-220.

V.257 Vase with one handle. 7.25"h x 6.5"w x 4.63"d. Backstamp: 27.1. $280-330.

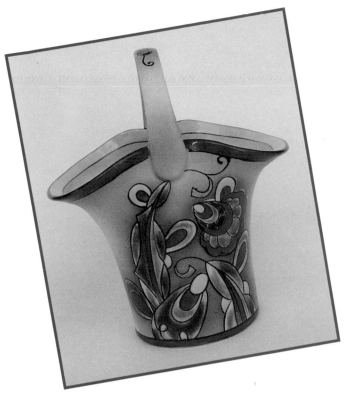

V.258 Vase with one handle. 7.25"h x 6.5"w x
4.63"d. Backstamp: 27.1. $230-280.

V.259 Vase with one handle. 7.25"h x 6.5"w x 4.63"d.
Backstamp: 27.1. $190-250.

V.258A Reverse of V.258.

V.260 Vase with one handle. 5.88"h x 7.75"w x
4.75"d. Backstamp: 27.0. $150-180.

V.261 Vase with two handles. 11.13"h x 6.0"w. Backstamp: 27.0. $230-270.

V.262 Vase with two handles. 11.0"h x 6.25"w. Backstamp: 27.0. $280-330.

V.261A Reverse of V.261.

V.262A Reverse of V.262.

V.263 Vase with two handles. 10.5"h x 5.5"w.
Backstamp: 27.0. $190-240.

V.263A Detail of V.263.

V.264 Vase with two handles.
10.0"h x 6.13"w x 5.75"d.
Backstamp: 27.0. $170-220.

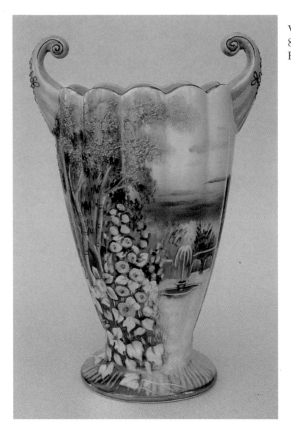

V.267 Vase with two handles.
8.25"h x 5.25"w x 3.5"d.
Backstamp: 27.1. $180-210.

V.265 Vase with two handles. 9.0"h x 5.75"w x
3.5"d. Backstamp: 27.1. $170-220.

V.266 Vases with two handles. 9.25"h x 4.5"w.
Backstamp: 27.0. Each, $110-130.

V.268 Vase with two handles. 8.25"h
x 5.25"w x 3.5"d. Backstamp: 27.0.
$120-180.

V.269 Vase with two handles,
signed H. Tanagi. 9.5"h x 4.5"w.
Backstamp: 33.056. $100-140.

V.270 Vases with two handles. 7.75"h x 3.5"w.
Backstamp: 25.1. Each, $100-140.

V.272 Vase with two
handles. 7.38"h x 3.88"w.
Backstamp: 19.1. $130-160.

V.271 Vase with two handles. 8.0"h x 6.0"w x 4.5"d.
Backstamp: 27.1. $190-240.

V.273 Vases with two handles. 7.0"h x 4.63"w. Backstamp: 27.0. Each,
$170-190.

V.274 Vase with two handles. 8.63"h x 7.0"w. Backstamp: 27.0. $170-190.

V.274A Reverse of V.274.

V.276 Vase with two handles. 6.5"h x 4.5"w. Backstamp: 27.0. $140-180.

V.277 Vase with two handles. 5.13"h x 4.13"w x 3.38"d. Backstamp: 19.1. $70-90.

V.275 Vase with two handles. 6.0"h x 5.0"w x 3.5"d. Backstamp: 27.0. $140-180.

V.278 Vase with two handles. 4.13"h x 7.38"w x 5.13"d. Backstamp: 27.0. $200-250.

V.281 Vase with three handles. 6.5"h x 4.0"w. Backstamp: 19.0. $120-170.

V.279 Vases with two handles, in original box. Vases, 3.0"h x 2.0"w. Box, 2.0"h x 4.38"w x 3.5"d. Backstamp: 27.0. As shown, $70-90.

V.282 Wall pocket. 8.75"h x 4.0"w x 3.0"d. Backstamp: 27.0. $210-260.

V.280 Vase with two handles. 3.0"h x 2.13"w. Backstamp: 27.0. $30-40.

V.283 Wall pocket. 8.75"h x
4.0"w x 3.0"d. Backstamp:
27.1. $210-260.

V.285 Wall pocket. 9.38"h x
3.25"w x 2.13"d. Backstamp:
27.1. $190-210.

V.284 Wall pocket. 9.38"h x
3.25"w x 2.13"d. Backstamp:
19.2. $190-210.

V.286 Wall pocket. 9.0"h x 4.25"w.
Backstamp: 19.0. $170-200.

V.287 Wall pocket. 8.25"h x 4.63"w x 2.63"d. Backstamp: 27.0. $190-250.

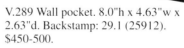

V.289 Wall pocket. 8.0"h x 4.63"w x 2.63"d. Backstamp: 29.1 (25912). $450-500.

V.288 Wall pocket. 8.0"h x 4.63"w x 2.63"d. Backstamp: 27.1. $170-200.

V.290 Wall pocket. 7.5"h x 4.5"w x
1.75"d. Backstamp: 27.1. $300+

V.291 Wall pockets. 5.88"h x 2.75"w x 1.63"d.
Backstamp (all): 27.1. Each, $50-90

V.292 Wall pockets. 5.88"h x 2.75"w x 1.63"d. Backstamp (all):
27.1. Each, $80-100.

Chapter Z

Miscellaneous Items

This chapter contains photos of the following miscellaneous Noritake-marked fancy line porcelains:

Crumb catcher (silent butler) (p.197)
Egg cup and warmer (p.198)
Grapefruit cup (p.198)
Napkin rings (p.199)
Place card holders (p.198)
Shaving mug (p.200)
Spooners (p.200-202)
Toast rack (p.202)
Toothpick holders (p.202)

Several of the pieces in this Chapter Z are quite impressive. An example is the place card holder set in the original box (Z.30). It is easy to see why the box is still around. Its utility for storage is obvious and considerable. The crumb catcher (or silent butler) in Z.26 is the only Noritake backstamped one I have seen thus far. I wonder, though, if a brush of some kind came with it originally. (Or maybe it is not a crumb catcher at all! But if not, then what is it?) And speaking of being complete, take special note of the small lid at the center of the egg warmer in Z.28. Hot water was put inside these items to keep soft-boiled eggs warm. The little lid, therefore, was quite important for it helped keep the water warmer longer and minimize spills. As you can imagine, though, such lids would be easy to lose or knock from a counter or table, so lidless versions of these items will be found. It is doubtful, however, that one would ever be able to complete such an item by finding just a lid somewhere.

Grapefruit cups are known to be a part of some Noritake dinnerware sets (Azalea, for example). Because the grapefruit cup in Z.29 is a lovely blue luster and has the backstamp it does (19.0), however, one is led to the (always tentative) conclusion that this piece was not part of a dinnerware set. It is, therefore, a rather unusual item in my experience, though perhaps not in yours. The napkin rings in Z.31 will be familiar to many Noritake collectors and, as the values indicate, they are sought after by many as well. They are a great Deco pair. Of at least as much interest, however, are the other fine napkin rings shown here (Z.32– Z.33) since they are quite a bit less common than one might think.

Spooners dominate the chapter, though, not only numerically but also in terms of overall design quality. Two fine Deco florals appear on Z.37 and Z.38, but the spooner with the most spectacular design is shown in Z.35. If you have looked at it, you will not need me to tell you what makes this piece so dramatic. It and a wonderful cigarette

jar in Chapter A (A.135) are far and away the most dramatic free-form geometric motifs I know of on Noritake fancy line porcelains. What is striking to many Noritake collectors is that such an amazing design should be lavished on such a humble piece as this double spooner. The optimists among us, however, like to think that this design on this piece points to the likelihood that there is, out there, an entire tea set with this motif, just waiting to be found by one of *us*. Dreams like this are what keep us all going. Enjoy and happy hunting to you all!

Z.26 Crumb catcher ("silent butler"). 1.75"h x 6.38"w x 4.5"d. Backstamp: 27.1. $50-90.

Z.26A Top view of Z.26.

Z.27 Egg cup. 2.5"h x 4.25"w. Backstamp:
26.0. $50-70.

Z.28 Egg warmer. 3.5"h x
5.63"w. Backstamp 27.0.
$130-150.

Z.29 Grapefruit cup. 3.63"h x
4.75"w. Backstamp 19.0. $70-90.

Z.30 Place card holders with original
box. Box, 1.63"h x 5.5"w x 3.63"d.
Holders, 1.5"h x 1.25"w. Backstamp
27.1. Set as shown, $190-230.

Z.31 Napkin rings. 2.63"h x 2.25"w. Backstamp 27.1. Each, $120-150.

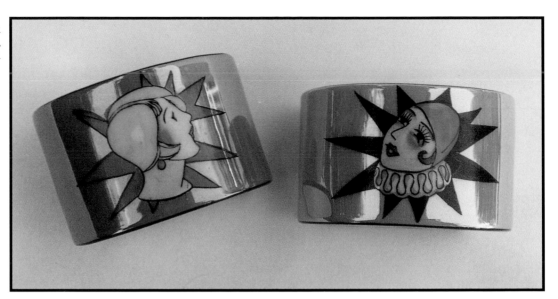

Z.32 Napkin rings. 3.13"h x 2.25"w. Backstamp 27.0. Each, $50-70.

Z.33 Napkin rings. 2.63"h x 2.25"w. *Left*, Backstamp 26.0. *Right*, Backstamp 27.1. Each, $30-50.

Z.34 Shaving mug (brush of the era, but not Noritake). 3.88"h x 3.88"w. Backstamp 27.0. $120-150.

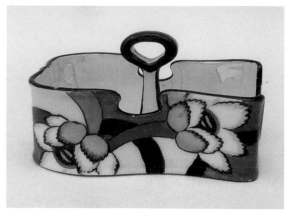

Z.37 Double spooner. 2.75"h x 4.88"w x 3.25"d. Backstamp 27.0. $80-120.

Z.35 Double spooner. 2.75"h x 4.88"w x 3.25"d. Backstamp 27.1. $190-240.

Z.36 Double spooner. 2.75"h x 4.88"w x 3.25"d. Backstamp 27.1. $90-130.

Z.38 Spooner. 2.38"h x 8.0"w x 1.88"d. Backstamp 27.0. $70-90.

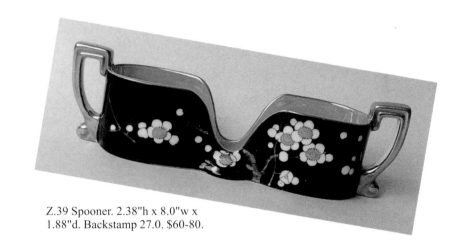

Z.39 Spooner. 2.38"h x 8.0"w x
1.88"d. Backstamp 27.0. $60-80.

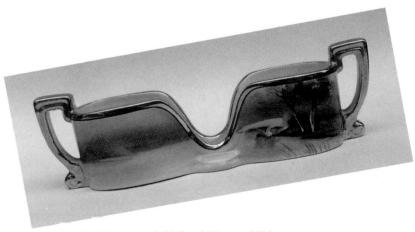

Z.40 Spooner. 2.38"h x 8.0"w x 1.88"d.
Backstamp 27.0. $50-70.

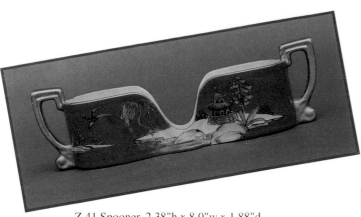

Z.41 Spooner. 2.38"h x 8.0"w x 1.88"d.
Backstamp 27.0. $60-80.

Z.42 Toast rack. 2.75"h x 5.13"w.
Backstamp 38.1. $50-80.

Z.43 Toothpick
holder. 2.0"h x
2.88"w. Backstamp
MIJ.1. $60-70.

Z.45 Toothpick holder. 2.0"h x 4.5"w. Backstamp
27.1. Each, $70-90.

Z.44 Toothpick holder.
2.0"h x 2.88"w. Backstamp
MIJ.1. $60-70.

Bibliography

Because the Bibliography was accidentally omitted from *Noritake, Collectibles A to Z* all items referred to in that book are included here, along with the items referred to in this book. In addition, selected sources on Art Deco, which were not mentioned specifically in the text (e.g., of Chapter 2, above), are included, sometimes with a few comments as to their relevance for readers of this book.

Alden, Aimee Neff , and Marian Kinney Richardson. 1987. *Early Noritake China: An Identification and Value Guide to Tableware Patterns*. Lombard, Ill.: Wallace-Homestead Book Company.

Arwas, Victor. 1976. *Art Deco*. New York: St. Martin's Press. (Small paperback, useful as a convenient and brief introduction to the subject by one of its acknowledged masters, but see next item.)

Arwas, Victor. 1992. *Art Deco*. New York: Harry N. Abrams, Inc., Publishers. (Art Deco has never been presented any better, visually, than it is presented in this big [and somewhat expensive] book. The photography is superb, the selections magnificent and the essay that accompanies all this is thoughtful and detailed. This book is a must for any serious collector of Art Deco Noritake.)

Ayars, Walter. 1990. *Larkin China*. Summerdale, Pa.: Echo Books.

Benedict, Ruth. 1934. *Patterns of Culture*. New York: Mentor Books (1959).

Donahue, Lou Ann. 1979. *Noritake Collectibles*. Des Moines, Iowa: Wallace-Homestead Book Company.

Duncan, Alastair. 1986. *American Art Deco*. New York: Harry N. Abrams, Inc., Publishers. (A *big* book with fine illustrations, but mostly in black and white. Of special interest for its emphasis on the American version of [modernist] Art Deco, but see also Weber, below.)

Duncan, Alastair. 1988. *Art Deco*. London: Thames and Hudson. (What this small book lacks in color illustrations [only 44 of the 194] it makes up for in the detailed and thought-provoking essay that runs throughout the book.)

Edward, Alfred W. 1996. *Art Deco Sculpture and Metalware*. Atglen, Pa.: Schiffer Publishing. (Good color photos of materials that tend to be given little attention in other more general books on Art Deco.)

Failing, Patricia. 1995. *Howard Kottler: Face to Face*. Seattle, Wash.: The University of Washington Press.

Gaston, Mary Frank. 1997. *Collectors Guide to Art Deco, Second Edition*. Paducah, Ky.: Collector Books. (A useful book for many collectors because it covers a wide range, includes values and has few "we'll never se 'em" "high end" items.)

Griffin, Leonard, and Louis K. and Susan Pear Meisel. 1988. *Clarice Cliff: The Bizarre Affair*. New York: Henry N. Abrams, Inc. (A very large format paperback with fabulous *large* photos of Cliff's designs which so clearly resonate with similar motifs on Noritake porcelains.)

Heide, Robert, and John Gilman. 1991. *Popular Art Deco: Depression Era Style and Design*. New York: Abbeville Press. (Emphasizes post-1920s works and, thus, may be somewhat less relevant to collectors of Art Deco Noritake. It is, however, an important work of value to serious collectors of Art Deco Noritake.)

Heller, Steven, and Louise Fili. 1995. *Streamline: American Art Deco Graphic Design*. San Francisco: Chronicle Books. (Beautifully designed book with a fine selection covering a great range of the relevant materials. Many examples will strike a responsive chord with collectors of Art Deco Noritake.)

Hida, Toyojiro. 1996. *Early Noritake*. Nagoya, Japan: The Noritake Company, publisher.

Hillier, Bevis. 1971. *The World of Art Deco*. New York: E. P. Dutton. (This is where it started, in the United States anyway: in 1971 at the Minneapolis Institute of Arts, and this is the book about not only that landmark exhibit but also about Art Deco as understood by Hillier. Black and white illustrations. Exhibit catalogue.)

Klein, Dan. 1974. *All Colour Book of Art Deco*. London: Octopus Books. (Great little book, undoubtedly out of print but worth hunting for in a used bookstore. Fine color photos of an excellent array of Art Deco items ranging from buildings to perfume bottles.)

Kottler, Howard. 1982. *Noritake Art Deco Porcelains*. Pullman, Wash.: Museum of Art, Washington State University.

Levie, Alison, translator (no author given). 1998. *French Art Deco Fashions in Pochoir Prints from the 1920s*. Atglen, Pa.: Schiffer Publishing. (A beautiful, lavishly illustrated book likely to appeal to all who collect Noritake "lady motifs," though none of the many illustrations in this book appear to have directly inspired any Noritake designs.)

Lobanov-Rostovsky, Nina. 1990. *Revolutionary Ceramics: Soviet Porcelain 1917-1927*. New York: Rizzoli. (This book beautifully covers an important subject for collectors of Art Deco generally and Art Deco Noritake in particular. Check it out!)

Marion, Frieda, and Norma Werner. 1979. *The Collector's Encyclopedia of Half-Dolls*. Paducah, Ka.: Collector Books.

McClinton, Katherine Morrison. 1986 (1972). *Art Deco: A Guide for Collectors*. New York: Clarkson N. Potter, Inc. Publishers. (All black-and-white illustrations but a very good and detailed essay runs through the entire book.)

McCready, Karen. 1995. *Art Deco and Modernist Ceramics*. London: Thames and Hudson. (Of all the books listed in this bibliography, this is probably the one that serious collectors of Noritake Art Deco porcelains should first consider adding to their library. It is well organized, jam-packed with information and shows some great Deco Noritake, including the fabulous "Jewels" bowl. In addition, there is a fine introductory essay on Art Deco by Garth Clark. This book is a must!)

Noritake Company, The. 1997. *Noritake: History of the Materials Development and Chronology of the Backstamps*. (Published anonymously by the Noritake Company.)

Spain, David H. 1994. "Searching for Art Deco and the Elements of a Style: A Personal Account." in Joan Van Patten, 1994, *The Collector's Encyclopedia of Noritake, Second Series*. Paducah, Ky.: Collector Books.

Spain, David H. 1997. *Noritake Collectibles, A to Z: A Pictorial Record and Guide to Values*. Atglen, Pa.: Schiffer Books.

Van Patten, Joan F. 1979. *The Collector's Encyclopedia of Nippon Porcelain*. Paducah, Ky.: Collector Books.

Van Patten, Joan F. 1982. *The Collector's Encyclopedia of Nippon Porcelain, Second Series*. Paducah, Ky.: Collector Books.

Van Patten, Joan F. 1984. *The Collector's Encyclopedia of Noritake*. Paducah, Ky.: Collector Books.

Van Patten, Joan F. 1986. *The Collector's Encyclopedia of Nippon Porcelain, Third Series*. Paducah, Ky.: Collector Books.

Van Patten, Joan F. 1994. *The Collector's Encyclopedia of Noritake, Second Series*. Paducah, Ky.: Collector Books.

Van Patten, Joan F. 1997. *The Collector's Encyclopedia of Nippon Porcelain, Fourth Series*. Paducah, Ky.: Collector Books.

Van Patten, Joan F. 1998. *The Collector's Encyclopedia of Nippon Porcelain, Fifth Series*. Paducah, KY: Collector Books.

Watson, Howard and Pat Watson. 1993. *Collecting Art Deco Ceramics*. London: Greenwich Press. (Superb range and fine color photos, including the Noritake covered box with the figural "seated lady" shown as part of a lamp base.)

Weber, Eva. 1985. *Art Deco in America*. New York: Exeter Books. (A beautifully illustrated book, though many photos not in color. "Jewels" is shown, in color.)

White, Carole Bess. 1994. *Collector's Guide to Made in Japan Ceramics: Identification and Values*. Paducah, Ky.: Collector Books.

White, Carole Bess. 1996. *Collector's Guide to Made in Japan Ceramics: Identification and Values, Book II*. Paducah, Ky.: Collector Books.

White, Carole Bess. 1998. *Collector's Guide to Made in Japan Ceramics: Identification and Values, Book III*. Paducah, Ky.: Collector Books.

Index

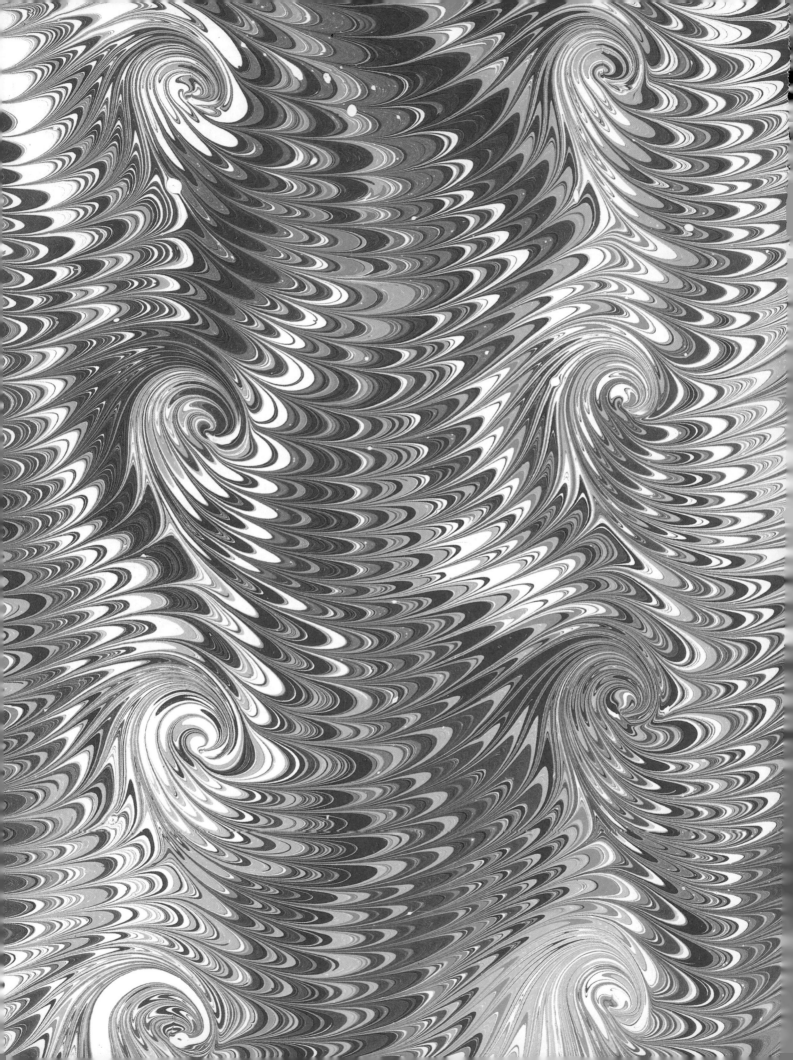